THE PATHLESS PATH

THE PATH OF LOVE

VIKAS VARMA

*This book has been inspired by and dedicated to Consciousness.
All names and forms are born from and merge into the
Consciousness. 'The Pathless Path', to experience the
truth of ourselves has emerged as a spontaneous flow
of Consciousness. Consciousness has revealed itself to
be the all-pervasive energy experienced by all beings
as love. The Pathless Path is the Path of Love.*

CONTENTS

INTRODUCTION

Ever since I became aware of my oneness with Consciousness, all its wisdom became available to me. As my *Guru* Sri Sathya Sai Baba had blessed, I began sharing this Direct Guidance through my writings, videos and weekly online sessions. A core group of earnest seekers on the journey of inner transformation began to attend the weekly sessions of "Infinite Love". They not only received the much-needed guidance but also individually experienced the energetic presence of Consciousness, that too on a video call across various continents and time zones.

At the end of one such call, on 29th October, 2022, one of our senior-most participants Mr. R.K. Palliwal inquired if it was possible for me to conduct a daily session. In his tone there was a sense of urgency to realise his true Self. He said, 'every day in my meditation I reach the Golden Gates of Consciousness but am unable to enter it. I have a strong feeling that you can get me inside. I don't know how much time I have left and I certainly want to experience the One Consciousness in this lifetime'.

My first instinct was to say 'no', for daily sessions seemed impractical and impossible. The next day it occurred to me that this request was from a sincere seeker, who is rare to find on this path. I recalled that Krishna had been on the lookout for a sincere seeker like Arjuna before he shared the priceless wisdom of 'Bhagavad Gita'. I realised that it was my *Dharma* (duty) to take a daily session for this earnest seeker. I sent a message announcing a call for the next evening, to discuss the requirements of all those who were interested to attend the daily sessions.

On the call of 31st October, 2022 only five persons turned up and I asked each one of them to share with me at least one question the answer of which they were still seeking. By the end of the call we had five questions and I realised these would take care of our first five sessions. I announced that we would start the daily sessions from the next day being 1st November, 2022.

On the morning of 1st November, I was guided by the Consciousness that these sessions were to be held for 40 days and they would be called *Atma Chalisa Parayanam.* The Consciousness announced that all those who would observe the 40-day *Parayanam* with full faith, fervour and dedication would experience Self Realisation. It was a tall claim to make especially when, at that time, I had no clue what we were going to cover during the 40 days. However, I have learnt not to question the ways of the Consciousness and to go with the flow.

As the program began the Consciousness began unfolding the plan to me and we started on a phenomenal journey on the Pathless Path of Love. On the first day there were only six participants. I figured that the numbers might reduce further as the days would progress. However, the Consciousness had other plans. The energetic presence started to reach out to other seekers whose time had come and by the time the program ended there were twenty-five participants from all over the world.

What transpired during the 40 days was miraculous. The transformation that people experienced was immense and the participants sharing became intense as the program progressed. I was happy when Mr. Palliwal shared after the program that he could freely enter the Golden Gates of Consciousness, and experience the flow of One Consciousness. I realised how Consciousness used Mr. Palliwal as an instrumental cause, for a once in a lifetime program, that had the power to transform millions of lives. We decided to share this program on YouTube so that it could reach the Universe of all seekers. The Consciousness then used another participant from Argentina, who saw this program as a book in her meditation. Thus, started an incredible journey of coming together of transformed hearts to bring to all of you this offering of love and light. It is 'The Pathless Path – the Path of Love'.

I acknowledge and convey my heartfelt gratitude to Palliwal Ji, Asha Ji, Deepti, Denise, Katarzyna, Mercedes, Philippa, Poonam, Raju, Shipra and Sonia for their valuable contribution in making this book possible in such a short period of time.

Vikas Varma

INTRODUCTION

A Participant's Perspective

Sometimes the best things in life come as a total surprise. The Pathless Path program which resulted in this book, was one of those surprises, it was a sudden unexpected gift from Consciousness. It all started at the end of 2022 during a weekly group call. That day, somebody asked Vikas what many of us would have loved, but never thought could have been possible. The question was whether we could meet daily to maintain the exquisite energy that was being transmitted on our calls. At the time, this seemed impossible with so many commitments at work and at home. Who would ever have the time? To add to that, we were a worldwide group and finding the right time for everybody to meet seemed impossible. However, a few days later, the program started and somehow, we agreed to give it a try. Consciousness through Vikas revealed to us that it would be a 40-day program leading to Self-realisation. The name given to the program was *Atma Chalisa Parayanam.*

Why 40 days? Well, in many religions this period is important as it takes 40 days to establish a new habit and to reprogramme our subconscious. Even Jesus spent 40 days and 40 nights in the desert as part of his spiritual journey. Each day Vikas would progressively share with us not only why we were born but also how to avoid having to go through the whole journey of life yet again. On that journey of birth to Self-realisation we also learnt how to play the game of life and to see things from a different perspective. In fact, life wasn't that difficult after all, the challenges were there for a reason and life was a preparation for something more brilliant than we could have ever imagined.

Many of us had been on a spiritual journey for many years, knew a lot of the theory and had followed other programmes. However, this time it was different, there was an inner transformation taking place at a pace that took us all by surprise. How was this possible? Well only Consciousness knows the full story. From our perspective, we felt a loving energy embracing us each day on the calls and as we contemplated that day's teachings.

Then a miracle happened; we started to gradually experience the knowledge which was being imparted to us. The inner Self started to emerge. Many of us also started experiencing a tranquil state of being and some even tapped into other dimensions. So, it was a combination of the tranquil state, the loving energy and experiencing the inner self which caused the transformation that creeped in gradually and noticeably. Before we knew it, we were on a journey like no other. Some of us experienced the changes early on while others took a bit longer.

However, everybody who was totally committed to the 40 days had some level of life changing inner transformation. One of us reached the goal in those 40 days which proved to us that it was possible in this time. He had full faith and devotion and achieved the goal. A true inspiration to the rest of us.

Ten days after the completion of the program, the sessions started to be made into videos. Amazingly, the loving energy could also be experienced from the videos. This was such a treat, as it allowed us to do the program again and reinforce our inner transformation. Each day, one session was shared on YouTube for all to see and experience. This is when others started to follow the program and those who consistently followed it on YouTube also started to experience an inner transformation. This was incredible as now the potential of the 40-day program was available to all seekers anywhere in the world. A platform for spreading the message of Consciousness had been established.

Then came the development of the Kailasalove.com website which included not only the 40-day program but all of Vikas Varma's abundance of videos and writings expressing the one Consciousness. Now everything was in one place for all to easily find and navigate through. It was at this stage that the 40-day program was named the Pathless Path Program. A path that treads so lightly that it doesn't leave any impression behind. A path that brings all paths together. A path that has no rigidity. A path that flows around all obstacles on the way. A path devoid of expectations and attachments. A path that is pure and selfless. A path that is full of sweetness and fragrance. A path so expansive that it carries everyone along. A path strewn with radiant light. A path that carries the breath of the Gods.

Just as the Pathless Path was established on the internet and other seekers started to join in, someone asked another unexpected question: Could this program be put into a book? The videos were all that was needed but the idea of being able to read it also was so enticing that we set out on another journey of giving birth to this book. This time though, many of the participants who had benefited from the program joined in the process. Some transcribed the videos, a few turned the transcriptions into the chapters in this book, Vikas finalised the text and others worked on the formatting of the book. Everybody used their skills or learnt new ones in this process of love in action. The spirit of loving collaboration was experienced by the group as everybody helped and encouraged each other in the process. This loving energy forms part of this book. Some of the team members who participated in the program and worked on the book have also shared their experiences.

To sum up, this book is not only brought to you by Consciousness but also by the collaboration of many seekers who have directly benefited from this program, whose only goal is to help the readers with their inner transformation.

Denise Furet - United Kingdom

FOREWORD

I am one of the fortunate people to have gone through the forty days Pathless Path Program, with great regularity and sincerity as a *Tapas* (rigorous spiritual practice) and as a *Yagna* (purificatory fire ritual).

Before undergoing this *Yagna*, despite all my spiritual efforts; reading many scriptures, listening to discourses of many saints, regular meditations, attending many *Satsangs*, *Bhajans*, *Nam Simran* sessions, service projects etcetera, I was only able to find my TRUE SELF in glimpses. All my earlier spiritual efforts had only resulted in self-purification.

In Vikas, I discovered the *Guru* who bridged the gap through this intense *Yagna* to finally land me in this limitless realm of deep peace and contentment. Since then, I am able to be with my TRUE Self where I dive now so effortlessly. It certainly is a choiceless mystical pathless path with no footprints, traversed by the SELF.

I gratefully admire the *Guru* in Vikas, who has facilitated the journey to the *Guru* within through this 40 days Pathless Path Program called the *Atma Chalisa Parayanam*. It is indeed a very well structured and systematic spiritual journey of forty days covering all aspects and facets a sincere seeker requires to accomplish his or her goal.

This intense *Sadhana* (disciplined spiritual practice) became a life changing event for me as the *Manana* (self-inquiry) after each day's episode cleared many mental blocks and unresolved issues.

Shri. R.K. Palliwal - India

FOREWORD

I thank the Divine Consciousness, which has been handholding me through its various forms ever since I consciously began to ask questions about life, doubting the material routines to be the be-all and end-all of its purpose. The journey on the path of discovering the Truth has been worth every breath, and the associated experiences, simply mind-blowing. As per the invisible and unknown divine plan, I was handed over from one *Guru* to the next until I was ready for the experiences of the world of the heart.

It was no fluke that I found myself saying YES to participating in the *Atma Chalisa Parayanam* even though every inch of my sane mind told me that it would be impossible to sustain through the entire 40 days, given my commitments and tight schedules. But, within, my heart yearned to walk to the other side of the bridge and step into the world of love and light. The Divine was surely aware of it, but does It ever divulge its script in advance? I was spellbound to experience how the Divine co-created the means to achieve this end!

This *Parayanam* unlocked the doors to a new way of knowing life, acknowledging it, and living it. From a closed and conditioned existence, which I mistook for an aware existence, it gave me the strength to open the windows and let the light of an unburdened, unconditioned existence awaken in me. I wondered when the penny would drop for me until one day, high up in the skies on my flight to Delhi, I realised that it was 'I', now and here.

It was the way in which the entire *Parayanam* happened that led me to believe in the Pathless Path. The Master himself was a practical example of all the lessons he was equipping us with. Observing him, I felt encouraged to take the first step into this journey on the unknown pathless path, the only familiarity being some terminology, which too was not needed the way this knowledge was handed. An experiential journey, so well guided and in the simplest manner, made understanding easy and relatable to daily life. The guided meditations, the clearing of doubts, and the unhesitant openness of the participants in sharing their experiences brought in a love energy that was beautiful, innocent, and sublime.

I, who was very uptight, also began to let go of my inhibitions, open up and share, and trust the master. He is no ordinary being; revelling in the ocean of love, he has the capacity to lead others to it and help them taste its sweetness. I shared an 'unconditioned love'-'conditioned love' relationship with him. He unconditionally loved my soul, yet I only conditionally loved him as long as he didn't prick my ego! But believe me, He really helped me to come out of my ego shell, into which I had withdrawn myself for want of protection, and armed me instead with the power of pure love to move on in my life. I see its magic and wonder at my own transformation!

After attending the *Parayanam*, the Divine unfolded its plan for a book on it, and I was asked to coordinate for the same, besides writing and editing. Well, everything that was part of my learning during the forty days of *Parayanam* was put to a quick practical test. As I set about it, the world of the mind once again began to colour the world of my heart into compartments of black and white. My work-oriented conditioning now became my new challenge, but the *Guru* was so beneficent that he came to my rescue every time I slipped and fell into my conditioned prison of the mind.

My team members were very nice people and genuine to the core, which made my task of coordination a cake walk. We were independent individuals working on the mission of getting this book ready. We were all working from the level of 'I'. And then the Divine gave a date for the release of this book. No sooner had this time frame appeared on our canvas of life, I saw most of us in the doldrums of 'possible'-'not-possible' play of the mind. We settled for the axiom: 'Let us do our best honestly and leave the rest to divinity. Slowly, the 'honesty energy' of each group member transformed into one collective love energy with all boundaries of individuality dissolving into it. The individual 'I' merged as 'we' in the love for the ultimate 'He'.

We clapped and cheered, we encouraged and energetically held hands, moving together to our destination of love. Even though physically we were all in various countries across continents, we were one energetically. The entire process of working on the book has given me the practical experience of 'Let go and flow' and in that flow I experienced the oneness, the love, and the joy that it brings with it. The bridge has been crossed, the first step into the world of the heart has been taken, and the meaning of synchronicities well understood. A prayer of gratitude escapes my lips, 'Thank you O' Gurudeva, for bringing me into this world of boundless love.'

Deepti Chopra - India

FOREWORD

What can I say about this journey that seemingly started some months ago, when Palliwal Uncle came up with the idea of this *Atma Chalisa Parayanam*? I am asked to write a few words about my experiences while participating, transcribing and editing, but how to describe them?

I could say this amazing and beautiful journey had quite a few hurdles, which helped me to focus my awareness on every thought, word and action. I could also say that, with each passing day, we moved deeper and deeper into that space of silence and stillness in our heart where we can listen to the inner prompting of Consciousness, which impels us to let go of the past and act from the centre of love and compassion in our heart in all circumstances. But these are words that very poorly describe the experience.

How can one put words to the wordless? How can one describe the love and oneness that flows and connects us to everyone and everything? I don't know whether this path of love is pathless, since many must have trodden it before us; but I do know without a doubt that it is a path that has no beginning and no end. It is endless, infinite, *Anant*.

I am profoundly grateful to Sathya Sai Baba, my Guru, my Father, my Mother, my best Friend and the Love of my life, for bringing us all together in this magic circle. I am in gratitude to dear Vikas for guiding us through these 40 days of *Parayanam* and to my fellow travellers for their love and their presence in this journey. I feel it was just the right time, the right place and the right people. I also feel like we have been travelling together since the beginning of time and we will continue travelling together into Eternity.

Good bless you all.

Mercedes Wesley - Argentina

FOREWORD

I had never met Vikas Varma but was introduced to his visualisations and meditations by a friend. They had left me transfixed in another realm, so when I heard about the 40-day experiential Self realisation program, I jumped at it. Day by day we were drawn into the Consciousness, led by Consciousness and experienced by Consciousness. My awareness became sharper, moments of clarity appeared and blissful snippets of peace and the opening of my heart occurred. Our sharing as a group clarified, explained and made me laugh and cry. So precious that company of hearts.

To my surprise, I was asked to do the editing as I was a complete novice. I obviously needed to concretise my understanding. At first the words were jumbled and unclear but the more I focused and sometimes walked away, they became clear and I understood the meaning, fantastic and I moved on to the next sentence. I learned to trust my intuition and have faith in the Consciousness within me. I found that each day the same subject appeared in the thoughts of the day or on the videos, no surprise there. To our wonderful mentor who patiently, tirelessly guided, explained, scolded and loved us and gave us the experience of a lifetime as promised, my eternal gratitude flows for ever.

Shanti, Shanti, Shanti.

Philippa Malcomson - United Kingdom

GETTING STARTED

There are 3 steps you need to follow when carrying out the Pathless Path Program.

1. Start with Day 1 and read each chapter one by one. It is advisable not to read more than one chapter a day. You can read the chapter at any time of the day or even several times a day.

2. You should take some time in the day to introspect on the knowledge given in the chapter and how it applies to you through a process of self-enquiry and/or self-audit. In Vedanta this step is call 'Manana'. Reading the chapter in the morning gives you more time in the day to do this important process.

3. Keep a Journal to take down notes while reading the chapter and later add your introspection. You should also refer back to your notes in order to build on your knowledge and introspection as you go through the program. This journal may be your friend for life.

Once you have completed all the chapters, we would love to hear your experiences. We also hold weekly calls for everybody who has completed the full program and is interested to continue on this journey of love and light. Please contact us via the contact page of our website at kailasalove.com

CHAPTER 1: SAT CHIT ANANDA 9 STEPS TO DIVINITY

We begin our forty-day journey on THE PATHLESS PATH by defining the steps that will serve as guideposts for realising our true Self. These have been compiled into a booklet titled 'Sat Chit Ananda – 9 Steps to Divinity', which came to light with the inspiration of Sri Sathya Sai Baba. I shall discuss these in detail here so that we are clear about the entire route in our sacred journey. It serves as a great checkpoint and an opportunity to evaluate our present state as we embark upon this journey today.Step

1 – Lamenting

As we move through our journey in life, several thoughts flood our mind leading to a plethora of unanswered questions. We often find ourselves lamenting about the struggle and futility of life. Some of the thoughts that often make us lament are

- 'When we feel that something is not right in our life
- When something is missing, and we don't know what it is
- When we feel a great void or emptiness in the midst of both success and failure
- When we feel restless in our mind
- When the pleasures of the world do not give us lasting peace and happiness
- When everything appears so artificial and unreal'

Adding a few more which are not in the book:

• When it feels that everything around us is falling away; when everything seems to be disintegrating

• When it feels that all problems are chasing us

• When it feels that all hell has broken loose

• When it feels like, 'Why am I being targeted by the Universal Consciousness?'

• When everything, one after the other, seems to be going wrong; everything seems to be scattering

We often lament, 'Why me?'. This kind of lamenting has either already happened to us or is happening to each one of us in the present. This, in fact, is the reason for our choosing this path. The good news is that, when such questions confront us, know that we have taken the first step to understanding our true Self or who we truly are. It is a pre-stage to the second stage which is the stage of Yearning or Seeking.

Step 2 – Yearning / Seeking

Having experienced the first stage, we automatically start to seek something which is missing, and this leads us to experience the following:• 'We experience an unknown voice calling us

• When we crave for authenticity

• When the heart pines to know the cause of melancholy – the sadness in our heart

• When the baffled mind yearns to know the missing link

• When we seek the source of everlasting happiness

• When the pursuit of truth about our Self becomes an obsession, know that we have progressed further'

Even though we do not know why things are happening to us, we want to find our answers and, therefore, we start seeking them. This is the second step in our journey towards reaching our own true Self, our Divinity.

For a lot of us, seeking happens intermittently. When we face challenges or the blows of life, or when we have serious spiritual questions, then we reach out to seek our answers, and once satisfied with them, we go back to our worldly routine again. We continue to remain in our ignorant mode of spiritual slumber. Again, after some years, tormented by more situations of life, we surface only to go back to the sleep mode in due course. This process continues until we truly become earnest spiritual seekers.

We go through the phase where we yearn and then something comes in, we get a few answers, feel happy about it and go back to our merry ways, till something else happens. This is part of the awakening process; it is a part of preparing us and it happens to each one of us. The one who really yearns with all his heart and soul, with a single-minded dedication, clearly is the one who gets it. *Seek and ye shall get.* This seeking is a fundamental and essential reason why there are some who make it. Baba used to say, 'There are millions who come to me, but I can count on the fingers of my one hand those who will get it or those who really seek me.'

So there have always been just a few who have chosen to go the whole way. The others get either distracted or become happy with whatever little trinkets they find on the way and therefore they are for some reason or the other unable to go the entire way. What is required is the devotion of an Arjuna, of a Nachiketa or of all those who went on to realise their Self because their yearning was so strong.

Step 3 – The Guru Arrives

Therefore, when this yearning becomes extremely strong, the third step automatically happens, which is when the *Guru* arrives. Know well that if there is an Arjuna, there is always going to be a Krishna!

'The intense seeking of the truth attracts the *Guru* (the wise one). He brings the light of knowledge of the Self and removes the darkness of your ignorance. The *Guru* is the embodiment of love and wisdom. The *Guru* inspires, guides, and guards you on the path of the truth of the Self. The authenticity and simplicity of the *Guru* draws you to him. The attraction is almost instant and magical. You experience an intense personal bond with your *Guru*. Despite your vulnerability, you feel safe and secure in the *Guru's* presence. This is the stage when you are now ready to follow the *Guru's* message.'

When we seek God, He comes to us in the form of a *Guru*. It is the intense yearning of the disciple that brings this *Guru* since he is always waiting for the disciple to get ready. We willingly expose our vulnerabilities, our weaknesses because we feel safe with our *Guru*. We start developing faith in the *Guru*. This faith is so essential in this journey because it gives us courage to go into an unexplored area or an uncharted territory. So, once the *Guru* arrives in our lives, we move on to the next stage which is regarding the message that the Guru brings.

Step 4 – The Message

True Masters are the embodiments of wisdom. This wisdom comes in the form of a message which is of prime importance. It is this message which removes the darkness of ignorance. It is this message which makes a *Guru* as a *Guru*, and it is this message that has the capacity to transform us. It is this message that has brought the *Guru*. The *Guru* comes in only as a messenger, a messenger of Consciousness. The *Guru* brings us that which is going to liberate us. This is the message that we have been waiting for. We are willing to receive this message from the *Guru* because, remember, by now we have built some kind of a relationship - we love the presence of this *Guru* and therefore are willing to listen to him. The message is available everywhere else as well, but we want to listen only to our *Guru*. So, what is the message?

'The *Guru* arrives as a redeemer and brings the message of Truth. The Truth about the reality of your Self, Creation, and the Creator which is:

• that the same one Divinity of the Creator pervades the entire Creation

• that the individual Self is none other than the manifestation of that Divinity

• man is verily Divine (God)- TAT TVAM ASI

• all things created are perishable, impermanent and subject to change, they are meant for your enjoyment, but they do not belong to you. Use and enjoy them without getting attached to them

• only the Divine Self is changeless, permanent, and eternal. This truth of your Self is referred to as SAT in the Vedas

Listening attentively to the message of the Guru is called *Shravanam*.'

Now, this message is the crux of our human experience. This is our Truth. This is what we are seeking. This is the message that is brought into our life. It takes us such a long time to get serious about this message and then to seek it and to move towards it; to try and invite this message; to try and live this message; to experience it first-hand and to become one with this message. Therefore, this message is what it is all about. As I said, the message must be brought into our lives by our *Guru* because it is the *Guru* who is the chosen one, who is the representative of God, who connects us to this truth, who connects us to this light within ourselves, who connects us to the Divinity, who brings us close to the very reason for our existence. This is the message of the *Guru*.

Step 5 – Self Inquiry (Mananam)

This message takes us to the next step because, having listened to this message, what we do with it is where the whole journey begins. Actually, we have a rebirth; we start living only once we start receiving this message because, before that, it's been a life of ignorance. When we awaken to this message, what we do with it will reflect as our progress on the journey. Simply knowing about this message will do nothing for us; we will remain where we are. We may become more erudite, we may become more scholarly, we may be able to debate, we may be able to argue, we may be able to convince others about the message; but we will not become the messengers of this message ourselves because this has just remained at an academic level. So, the fifth step is the step of self-inquiry or *Mananam*.

'The message of your inherent Divinity comes as a shock to your deeply conditioned mind. Doubts and questions arise in your mind and the inner dialogue starts.'

For a long time we had been living a different life, and now suddenly the *Guru* says that 'You are Divine, you are the Creator, everything is inside you'. Yet, at the same time, we are seeking it from outside, from a Guru; this whole contradiction starts to hit us. Doubts and questions arise leading to an unsorted inner dialogue. We begin to seek more clarity on, 'How is it possible?' This clarity comes to us when we use books of knowledge and inspiration which we call scriptures. We start studying these books by ourselves. We read the works of saints and sages like Paramhansa Yogananda, Swami Rama, Swami Chinmayananda, Sathya Sai Baba and other great Masters. This self-study is called *Swadhyaya*. 'More study and reflection bring more clarity and in the depths of silence you contemplate on the Divinity within. This stage is called *Mananam* or Self-inquiry. Your hunger grows and you seek the company of like-minded people. The company of seekers of truth or *Satsanga* helps you to overcome your doubts and confusion. You feel comforted that you are not alone in this quest of seeking truth. It emboldens you further and you discover a newfound courage to pursue the path less travelled.' This leads us to the next step on our journey.

Step 6 - Experience

'The teachings of the Guru and scriptures become synthesised and integrated in you. This is known as *Nididhyasana*. It is the process of freeing the mind from the clutches of its conditioning or ignorance. You completely understand that the 'Lord of life' is within you. However, knowledge can transform into wisdom only on the touchstone of direct experience which is called *Pratyakshya Pramana* or *Pratyakshya Anubhava*. Truth of the Self can be known only by putting into practice the teachings that have been listened to, contemplated, and synthesized. It requires patience, self-confidence and most importantly faith in the Guru to walk the path of your Truth. However, as you practice, all doubts vanish and wisdom dawns.'

Remember that the doubts and questions that we have are only until this stage because we have not yet practiced. It is very much possible that *Mananam* and *Swadhyaya* may not provide you with answers to your doubts but, once we practice, we will get direct evidence, direct experience, and all those doubts as well as questions will begin to go away. There is nothing like direct experience.

'It is then that the inner *Guru* reveals itself; the darkness of ignorance is removed by the light of wisdom and faith gives way to a deep sense of knowing. You seem to know or perceive things intuitively.'

Faith is the most significant starting point on this journey because, without faith in our *Guru*, we will never move forward. We may get too scared to go on to this less travelled path, but when we have faith in our *Guru*, our guide, we will feel encouraged to take the right steps.

However, it is important to note that if we keep asking questions to our *Guru* all the time, we would be making our Guru into a crutch. This implies we are getting addicted to the Guru, we are getting attached to the *Guru*. We are becoming lazy because we are not trying to see things for ourselves. Therefore, at a certain point of time the *Guru* will actually cut those ties, cut that attachment, because he knows that otherwise the disciple just becomes over-dependent on the *Guru*, always trying to get easy ready-made answers.

This path is our own journey. The *Guru* is always there around us; the *Guru* always surrounds us; the presence is always there, but each one of us has our own journey. We have to do it ourselves. The *Guru* cannot do it for us; our spouses, our friends, our children, cannot do it for us either. Life is a Do-It-Yourself program. It cannot be outsourced; it cannot be achieved on anyone's behalf by the *Guru*. It is our own journey and we alone have to take the steps. Hence, the need for direct experience!

It is important for us to understand the path of *Shravana*, *Manana*, and *Nididhyasana*. These are the three steps of learning and gaining expertise in any field of knowledge, be it the knowledge of the Self or the knowledge of any other thing. This then takes us to the seventh step towards experiencing our own Divinity and that is called Realisation.

Step 7 – Realisation

'Your experience prompts and propels you further on the path of your innate Divinity. The outside world loosens its grip on you and you experience intense detachment. Unexpected doors open and the direction of your life changes. Silence becomes golden and meditation becomes your friend. You start enjoying the journey of inner exploration. You experience a reservoir of Love, Light, and Joy within. You spontaneously start sharing this treasure with others. Giving brings great joy. Selflessness makes you loving. As you become more loving, people get attracted towards you. You discover the missing link and experience that the source of peace or *Shanti* is within you. You intuitively realise that it is the experience of the truth of your being. You are that Divine Consciousness that pervades and permeates the entire creation- *Aham Braham Asmi.'*

This is the point where we have a realisation for the first time of our Self, of our true nature- *Aham Brahamasmi* but it may not be a permanent experience. It leads us to the eighth step which is called Awareness.

Step 8 - Awareness

'Awareness is the key to transformation. The awareness of your Divinity brings about radical changes in your life. Your thoughts, words, and actions get aligned. This is called *Trikaran Shuddhi*. A life of authentic living starts. The melancholy in your heart ends. You clearly hear and understand the voice of your Consciousness. The seeking ends and you feel complete. You experience a sense of newness. NOW or the present moment is all that matters to you. You just want to BE. No more goals to achieve. You feel content (*Santosh*) and satisfied at all times.'

This is the second indicator of our state of awareness. The first one is peace (*Shanti*) and the second is contentment (*Santosh*).

'You become aware that the body and all its experiences are temporary and unreal. All these experiences happen in your awareness, and awareness is nothing other than the Atman. You experience that the truth of your Self is none other than the Creator and that this Creator is changeless and eternal - *Ayamatma Brahma* (one of the four Universal Truths in the journey towards experiencing *Ananda*). You remain in the awareness of this reality at all times (*Stitha Prajna*). This 'Constant Integrated Awareness' is referred to in our scriptures as *Chit*.'

We've spoken about *Sat* which is the truth of the Self and *Chit* is this 'Constant Integrated Awareness'.

Step 9 – Bliss

'Life becomes a flow. A flow that is natural, spontaneous and effortless- *Saral* and *Sahaj*. You experience overwhelming love for all. Selfish living gives way to selfless living. Love becomes service. You experience that you are the embodiment of love. You realise that Love is God and God is Love. Living becomes joyous. This joy becomes a constant. And this constant ever-present joy is the state of bliss or *Ananda*.'

So this journey of *Sat Chit Ananda* -the knowing of this truth, experiencing it directly, remaining in the awareness of it- is what gives us this bliss. Our life becomes an effortless flow. We remain a witness. All that is created by man is impermanent, transient, and temporary. Therefore, we remain as a witness which is ever present; which is all; which is also witnessing the mind and its shenanigans but is not involved with it. This awareness at all points of time brings us constant ever-present joy called *Ananda*.

That brings us to the close of Chapter one. With this we have set the context of what we are going to do and where we are starting from for the journey on THE PATHLESS PATH – THE PATH OF LOVE!

Prayers

The book ends with a prayer – 'May you revel in your Divinity and experience the same Divinity in every being and everything in creation.' This implies that not only shall you experience your own Divinity but once you do that, you shall experience the Divinity in every being and everything in creation. And 'May all experience uninterrupted and everlasting Bliss – *Sat Chit Ananda.'*

> *'Asato Ma Sad Gamaya (O Consciousness   lead us from Unreal to Real)*
> *Tamaso Ma Jyotir Gamaya (From Darkness to Light)*
> *Mrityor Ma Amrtam Gamaya.' (From Mortal to Immortal)*

Actually, these nine steps are nothing but the steps in the journey of moving from the unreal to the real which is the truth, *Sat*, and removing the darkness of ignorance by bringing in the light of awareness. This awareness makes us immortal, makes us one with that permanent truth of who we truly are; which is the key to liberation, the key to *Ananda*.

> *'Samastha Lokah Sukhino Bhavanthu*
> *Samastha Lokah Sukhino Bhavanthu*
> *Samastha Lokah Sukhino Bhavanthu*
> *Om Shanti Shanti Shanti'*
>
> *(May All Beings in All Dimensions be Happy. Om Peace Peace Peace)*

CHAPTER 2: GOAL OF LIFE

In Chapter 2, we discuss the Goal of Life. For any journey, one must have a goal in mind, failing which we will not reach anywhere. So, for our 40-day journey on The Pathless Path *(Parayanam)*, as well as our journey of life, we must have a clear goal in mind. Fortunately for us, the goal of life is also the goal of this *Parayanam*, i.e., *Atma Sakshatkara* or Self-realisation.

Such an event can take place only when the time is right and with the grace of the all-merciful, all-powerful, all-benevolent God. It's only with divine will *(Sankalpa)* that we can undertake such a practice. It requires from each one of us 40 days of intense immersion in our own selves. We would be going deeper and deeper into the Self, till we not only experience it, but we also experience what the experience means. No words and no language can ever define what *Ananda* (Bliss) is really like. Once we experience it, it cannot simply be put in words. Therefore, what we have set out to do is to have our own direct experience.

So, what is this goal that we are seeking from these 40 days and from our life? The Upanishads have laid it out for us. My *Guru*, Sai Baba, has emphasised it again and again and defined it as the goal of experiencing the Inner Self. To experience the Divine Consciousness within ourselves that pervades everywhere, to experience that Divinity and to remain in that Divine Consciousness, is the goal of our life.

The ultimate pinnacle of human consciousness is to experience the all-pervading Universal Consciousness. That is where the game ends; that is where the experience in this dimension ends. As souls, we are eternal. We are part of this Universal Consciousness. We come here, we take birth again and again only to be able to experience this goal, to be able to experience the presence of Divine Consciousness within us and without us, and to always remain in the experience of this Consciousness. Once we achieve this goal, this game of human life is over because we merge back to the source from which we came. We become one with this Divine Consciousness. And once that oneness is achieved, then we say that this round of continuous birth and death at the dimension of the earthly plane comes to an end. The One Consciousness then moves into other realms.

So, let's just focus on this particular realm and be clear why we are here. Once we have achieved this clarity and once each one of us decides for ourselves that this is our goal, then we can truly start taking small steps in the journey within. The beautiful thing about this journey is that we are going to travel far and wide, but we are not going to go anywhere outside. We are just going to explore the space within us. We are going to experience the depths of nothingness, because the Divine resides in the cave of our heart. There is a cave in the void that exists within each one of us. It is that journey that we are about to undertake.

Preparation is required by us to undertake this journey and the first step that we are taking today, which is a very important step, is to be really clear on the goal. If we look back at our lives, so far, each one of us has had a lot of experience in this particular lifetime. I'm not talking about experiences of past lifetimes but, in this lifetime, we've had many things that have been guiding us. We have been distracted in our lives, we have tried to run after multiple goals and, after all the experiences that we've had, we have all come to a point where we found something was missing in our lives. So, we've been trying to find that peace and contentment that we spoke about on day one. In search of that peace in our journey of life, we came to our *Guru*, and the *Guru* led us to his message. Therefore, what we are essentially seeking is the experience of *Aham Brahmasmi* - that the entire *Brahman* is my own Self. This, then, is the experience we seek as a very clear Goal.

The Goal of Self-realisation has been referred to by the Vedas as the highest and noblest goal of human existence *'Atmano mokshartham jagat hitaya cha'*, that the best service you can do for the whole world is to realise your own Self. One person transformed can help transform thousands who come into his or her influence, because light is something which does not diminish when shared. Light is the only thing which keeps expanding. That is why Sathya Sai Baba said that light is expansion and love is that light which expands.

If the goal is clear then it is easy to achieve it. As they say, 'Well begun is half done'.

Useful Tips

I would like to share a few other things that might be helpful during these 40 days. It would be good for each one of us to keep a journal to take notes for each chapter. Especially note down all the experiences you're having during the day because these experiences are going to shift. Remember, this is an experiential journey that we are undertaking and it will give you tremendous insight as you start going back over your experiences. I strongly feel this journal is going to become very handy for you, not only in these 40 days but thereafter as well.

It would be great if you can practice whatever is being discussed during these 40 days. Bring this to your awareness every morning. The acronym BABA is leaping out to me - Be Aware Be Alert. It may be a good idea to note down what your current level of awareness is and also the current level of your alertness. Everyday keep writing down for yourself how this alertness and this awareness is beginning to shift, because it will definitely shift.

Another thought that comes to me is from the

Upanishads, which says *'Shraddhavan labhate jnanam'* - the ones who are devoted, the ones who are fully into something, they are the ones who finally succeed and get all the knowledge. Today is such an important day in our journey, so we must take it upon ourselves that 'no matter what, I am going to achieve my goal at the end of 40 days'. And if we keep reminding ourselves of this goal, I can assure you that it is going to be experienced and we are going to reach it.

Parayanam is not just the repetition of something. It means being marinated in the spirit of God at all times'. If we can remain steeped in the awareness of the *Atma* for 40 days, then there is no reason for us all not to become one with that. The only thing we need to do is to remain in the Consciousness that 'I am that *Atma*'. It is through this *Atma* that we see, that we speak, that we hear. It is this *Atma* which is the controller of this body. It is this *Atma* which experiences and it is this *Atma* which has brought us all together. 40 days is such a strong period because all faiths and religions have effectively tested that, after 40 days of continued effort on a particular thought or idea, that actually manifests in our life. So, if we all can remain in the awareness of the *Atman* and attribute to the *Atman* whatever experiences we have, there is no reason why that will not manifest in us.

So, today is the day of making our goal clear. Tomorrow onwards, we will start to work from this important foundation. Please keep doing *Mananam* (contemplation) and writing your journal.

CHAPTER 4: BELIEVE

The next step is to have a firm belief in the goal of life. We must believe with our mind, heart and soul that the goal of life is to experience Divine Consciousness. Everything we achieve in our life is because we have a clear goal. Climbing Mount Everest is a clear goal. Seeking it intensely is a step required in preparation to reach the goal. We must believe that the goal is worth achieving and that we can achieve it. How do we get this conviction? How do we believe that is the goal of life?

This is where faith comes in. We either have faith in a *Guru*, or in God, or in our religion, or in our scriptures. All of them have spoken of that one God, of that God within us. From there, we have a strong belief that this goal is the correct one. So, this is the goal that we have taken for life. What about the goal that we have put for ourselves, that in 40 days we are going to achieve Self-realisation? We must fully believe that we are going to experience our own Divinity within these 40 days. I am not saying that it will happen on the 40th day; it can happen anytime between now and when we end.

The essential ingredient and the guiding force during this process is that we must BELIEVE. In this case, we are believing that it can be done, we are believing in ourselves, in that 'I will do it'. At least for these 40 days, have faith in your guide, who in this case happens to be me. If only for these 40 days, have the firm belief that you will be well guided to where you need to be. This belief is important because, if this belief is not there, if you have doubts, if you are not sure about the goal, about your own self or about your guide on this journey, you will falter.

Imagine we are a climber who decides to climb up Mount Everest. First, we have to believe that we can do it. Then, we have to believe that our equipment is strong enough and finally we have to believe in the guide, the *Sherpa* or the expert climber who is going to lead us in that climb. Right? If any of that is missing, then we cannot make this journey. In the same way, we must have firm faith and belief in ourselves, in our abilities that, 'Yes I'm going to do all that it takes and I will reach my goal.' Therefore, we must believe in the goal itself, in the guide who is going to help us to get there and in ourselves. If any of these are missing, then we are sure to fall flat on our face, we are not going to get there.

You must be wondering why I am spending so much time on all these preparatory steps. It is because I have learnt, and I am bringing to you all that the Universal Consciousness is guiding me to share. It's a synthesis of my journey, of my understanding, of my experience that, if this foundation is not there, we simply cannot move forward. And that is the reason why many try to climb Mount Everest but only a few succeed. Many of us seek Self-realisation but few get there. It's only because of lack of preparation, lack of belief, lack of intensity. These are fundamental, and I can't emphasise enough how important it is for each one of us to be absolutely crystal clear of what we are about to do. This journey is not for the faint-hearted, it is for the soul who is ready and whose time has come. This invitation has come from the Divine Consciousness. I believe that it is also coming from inside of you, because inside of you is the same Divine Consciousness as outside of you. It is that one Consciousness which is bringing us together. We must believe in all this.

These are not idle words. I'm not saying things for the sake of saying them, but because I believe in every word. I believe in this Pathless Path. I believe that we are in for a Divine treat, an experience of a lifetime. I don't use words unless I fully invest in them. My heart and soul, my energy, my emotions, my thoughts, my words and my actions are completely synchronised at this point in time. These words come from the depths of truth because, at an individual level, there is nothing left. Everything is flowing from there, and we are mere instruments through which this Consciousness flows. As the words come out, the Consciousness also speaks energetically to each one of us and our hearts receive these words. All is received by the corresponding energy of Oneness, which resides deep inside each one of us. Therefore, this faith is built upon our experiences.

There are four stages in this process. The first is belief. Belief is when we hear from others about the power of something; either the power of a Master, or of the Scriptures or of Divine Consciousness. We start believing because somebody close to us whom we respect tells us about something and we start believing in it, since it comes from a credible source. Then, we start to investigate that information. Later, through the information we have received, we have a first-hand experience and, when that experience comes, the belief turns into faith. Now it is not something that we have just heard; it is something that we have directly experienced ourselves. So, BELIEF plus EXPERIENCE is equal to FAITH. Faith further transcends into a stage which is called KNOWINGNESS. In faith, there is still some duality; you have faith in someone, in something or in some idea. There is also a chance that this faith is coming from something happening to you from the outside.

Therefore, we start having more and more faith and, as we start to experience the results of that faith, we come to a point which is called KNOWINGNESS. We start to know things because we know that, every time we do this, we get this result. So, FAITH plus DIRECT EXPERIENCE (Pratyaksha Pramana) is equal to KNOWINGNESS. This gives us the further experience that there is no other. We are One. This is called BEINGNESS, where there is no mind left. Effortlessly, we start experiencing the truth of our own reality, our own Self, in the state of BEINGNESS. So, BELIEF plus DIRECT EXPERIENCE is equal to FAITH; FAITH plus DIRECT EXPERIENCE is equal to KNOWINGNESS and KNOWINGNESS plus DIRECT EXPERIENCE gets us to the state of BEINGNESS. By then, all duality has merged, everything is only ONE and, therefore, we exist in that state of BEING.

A small and a necessary foundation of belief is very critical on this journey, and we will keep picking this up as we go through this experience. Remember, the one common thing that I've spoken about in all these stages of evolution is EXPERIENCE, and these are 40 days of DIRECT EXPERIENCE. We will experience it! It is an experiential journey. It is the evolution of our BELIEF into FAITH, into KNOWINGNESS and into BEINGNESS. So, the starting point is essential: belief in oneself, belief in a *Guru,* in a guide, and belief in the goal itself. We must check all these points which are called 'points of entry'. These are the base camp, the preparatory steps. If we are solid in our footing, in our understanding, in the intensity of our desire to be there, and if we believe that we are going to be guided properly and make the effort, it shall definitely happen. So, that is what I had to share with you today regarding this important step of the preparation for our journey.

CHAPTER 5: EXPERIENTIAL LEARNING

We are stepping into Chapter 5 which is about Experiential Learning. The Vedas have given us a very beautiful way of acquiring knowledge of the Self, the highest knowledge of our being, the highest knowledge of existence. They talk about experiencing the Self, and have given us the methodology of an experiential way of learning. This is the method that we will employ to achieve our goal.

This method is something that I have been applying to almost every facet of my life, be it teaching or learning. I found this method to be so holistic that it applies to almost all fields of knowledge. So, what is this method? The first step of this experiential method is called *Shravana* (to listen). Listening is different from hearing. Hearing is when we are not paying much attention to what is being conveyed, whereas listening happens when we give our whole attention to it. *Shravana* is listening to understand, listening to the knowledge that is being passed on to us either through the written word in books of sacred knowledge or by listening to the words of a teacher, a Guru or whoever is providing us with the knowledge or information.

Shravana can also be used for internal listening. We keep listening to the wisdom from various teachers, but the Teacher of all teachers is inside each one of us, the inner *Guru*. That inner *Guru* speaks to us through intuition and not through words or any spoken language. Over a period of time, we develop the ability to listen to the language of our inner *Guru*.

Shravana truly means to listen exactly as is being expressed by the teacher, without employing any kind of internal filter. Usually, when we listen, we have some biases and prejudices, some opinions and judgments, and we have a certain understanding of our own. So, when a teacher is providing us with some information or knowledge, we often tend to hear it based on our own convenience and perception. But when we listen with an open mind and not with a mind which is full of its own opinions, then it is called *Shravana*. That is the deeper understanding of *Shravana* - the first step from where our journey of experiential learning begins.

Once we have listened with an open mind to what the teacher is saying, the next step is called *Manana,* which means self-inquiry, reasoning or reflection. We now analyse in our mind whatever we have heard. We reason it out and try to go deeper into it. This is where we start to churn what we have listened to and also look at every facet of what has been heard. Many times, our prejudices, our judgments or our own earlier experiences start to create doubts or a different understanding, as opposed to what the teacher is telling us. This may be because most of the scriptures and Masters speak in parables; they never speak directly. Thus, an understanding of the meaning to the words of the Master is essential.

It is important for us not to jump to conclusions when we do self-inquiry, but to seek out the Master or teacher and clarify the doubts that we have. Another way of clarifying our doubts can be through reading books. This is called *Swadhyaya* (self-study). We try to corroborate what we have listened to or endeavour to remove our doubts by reading relevant books. These may either be the ones recommended by our *Guru* or those we feel internally or intuitively inclined to read. Therein we will find the necessary information to resolve our doubts. This too is a part of self-inquiry (*Manana*) because we are trying to clarify our understanding about what we have listened to during *Shravana*. *Swadhyaya* is a part of *Manana*.

In the Vedantic language, *Manana* is often referred to as the chewing process. When a cow is offered some fodder or grass, it chews it for a long period of time to improve digestion. Similarly, *Manana* is the chewing action, the process of analysis or reasoning that aids experiential learning thereafter.

Vedantic learning is based on reasoning, on asking questions and on having doubts. It does not force things on people. The Vedas were taught on the basis of the experiential truths being brought out, and a dialogue would happen in a *Gurukula* (residential school of holistic education). This is the area where the teacher and the students would live together. *Manana* was considered very important by our *Rishis*, seers and sages, because they knew that this wisdom could only be imbibed by the disciples after they had done their own self-inquiry and became convinced about the information and knowledge being given to them.

The third step is actually the most important step, which is the natural culmination of step one and two, and it is called *Nididhyasana*. In Vedantic terminology, *Nididhyasana* is the assimilation of the teaching to such an extent that we become embodiments of that knowledge. This is only possible by refining *Manana* to its best. In other words, it is the refinement of the understanding of Truth, as given by the Master, to the extent that we begin living it in practice.

Knowledge learnt is of no use if we do not put it into practice in our life. Gaining knowledge and clarifying and removing our doubts amounts to building conviction behind the learning, which gives us confidence to go ahead and practise it. It is only by practising that we will know if it is what we understood it to be, if what our *Manana* gave us is true or not. Practice is the final touchstone for us to know directly whether it works or doesn't work. If it does, then the teaching no longer remains external to us; we become the teaching itself. If not, we go back into the entire process again to gain more clarity and conviction so as to become one with the knowledge. This was the path given to us by our *Rishis*; this is how they taught everything.

Personal Experience

I have personally experimented with this in my life. When I first came in touch with Sathya Sai Baba, I realised that Baba had this ability to make things extremely simple. He would put complex ideas into very simple language, and they would really appeal to me. Back then, when I was in a *Samiti* (group), I was made the person in charge of what we used to call a 'Study Circle'. Every week, we would get together in the study circle, choose a topic and discuss it. Very soon, I found that everybody would come, bring the teachings of Baba and just repeat them. I used to think that we were behaving like parrots; we were just remembering His teachings and repeating them, each one trying to show how good an orator they were, or how well informed they were. But I found that there was no experience coming through. I did not want to be just like a parrot; I did not want to show everybody how much knowledge I had. Within four months, I left. When asked the reason, I said, 'I want to live these teachings and not just talk about them'.

So, what I did, I used to pick up one thing that I would like from what Swami said and I would do *Manana* on it. Daily, before retiring to bed, I would share my learning and understanding of it with my wife and, on the very next day, we would start practising (living) that teaching. While my wife would have issues in truly living the teaching, she noticed that I would get to practise them without any inner conflict or challenge. She even commented, 'You are moving and changing so rapidly, I don't even know who you are at all!' She would also say, 'How is it that you do not take any time to start practising it, while I find it so difficult to convince myself?'

I would encourage her by reminding her that, 'There are no rights and wrongs in this world. Life is just a big experiment; it is such a big stage. The whole world is a playground and we come here like children to play in it. So, if I am going to be restricted by my own mind, my opinions, my own judgments and what the world has told me, then I'll never progress. I have faith in my Master. I have absolute faith in Sri Sathya Sai Baba and His teachings. These particular words of His I completely agree with. Now, whether it works for me or not, the only way to find out is by practising it. So, I am just trying to figure out what He actually means. We should always remember that there is no harm, there is nothing at stake. Life is not a serious business. In life, we have come to reach the highest level of Consciousness. And if we are so blessed to find a teacher who has the ability to take us to that Truth, why would anyone want to let it go?'

When I met Baba, I knew that I had found the Teacher of all teachers, and I was not going to let that opportunity go to waste. He said, 'My life is my message'. I said, 'My life will be Your message as well, because I'm going to start practising'. So, I left the 'Study Circle'. I didn't want to interact with all those people who were very smart and had a lot of knowledge. Instead, I wanted to be a practitioner. So, slowly I got into this habit of 'One thought a day or one thing that appealed to me'; and I would think and analyse, read and try to clear my doubts about it. When I would feel reasonably assured that I had understood it, I would say, 'Okay let me try it. If it doesn't work it doesn't work, but if it works it would be fantastic!'

This faith, this openness to try and learn should be exactly the same as when we wanted to learn how to walk when we were young and knew only how to crawl. We trusted our mother, we trusted the grip of her hand, we trusted that she would not let us fall, and thus we learnt to walk. Similarly, for other activities in our life, be it learning to ride a bike or to swim, we barely ever got it right at the first attempt. If we really wanted it, we trusted the teacher, the process and the knowledge enough to practice diligently until we got it right. Setbacks and bruises may have been a part of acing it, but were never our deterrents.

So, the magic *Mantra* (Chant or spell) is 'Practice, Practice and Practice'; and there will be something beautiful waiting for us at the end of this practice. Let go of all the doubts, let go of all the fears and be like a child who wants to experiment with this world, who has no clue, who just has this openness and curiosity and wants to go and try everything out.

I was like that child. I took my time to decide to have faith in my Master, my Guru; and once I had that faith I was willing to try all that He was telling me to do. And not for a day have I regretted it! Even as I was open to my Master, I was never close to any other Master. I was open to receive what Maharishi Ramana had to say about Advaita Vedanta. I was open to hear what Swami Rama had to say about the Himalayan tradition of Masters. I was open to hear what Osho had to say in his own inimitable style of explaining the same Advaita Vedanta. I was open to any Master from whom I could learn something. I never said NO to anyone, because all Masters have their own way of explaining the same truths and we don't know in which way we are going to understand, because everyone is Divine. Once we become more and more open, we slowly start developing the ability to discriminate.

So, this is how these three steps of *Shravana, Manana, and Nididhyasana* worked for me and how I am using them to teach not only Vedanta but also other subjects. I have taught six different subjects, none of which I had learnt or studied before, and yet I have ended up teaching them effectively because I adopted the approach of *Shravana, Manana, Nididhyasana* to every learning. With that, I have found great success in being able to not only learn myself, but to teach, guide, and share with people effectively.

Today we have finished the groundwork. Our beautiful goal of Self-realisation is also given by the Vedas as '*Atmano mokshartham jagat hitaya cha*', that the best service you can do for the whole world is to realise your own Self or to get *Moksha*. A Self-Realised person is an asset to the society as he or she inspires many others on the path. It is such a noble goal to have for our life. It is such a worthwhile thing to have and to go for. If we truly believe that we have come for this purpose, if we truly believe that we can do it, if we truly believe in our guide for these 40 days, and if we truly remain committed for this period of time, then each one of us will truly get the results at the end of it.

If we are shaky or have doubts, if we have questions and if we think we are busy and cannot find time, then, too, it is fine. Vedanta is very patient, it waits; it waits for everyone until they are ready.

This is an experiential journey, everything learnt must be practised. If we are ready to honestly practise it, then the Divine is ready to present itself to us from within.

CHAPTER 6: POWER OF SATSANGA

Satsanga is one of the prime requisites on our journey to Self-realisation. *Sat* means truth and *Sanga* means company. So, literally *Satsanga* means 'the company of truth'. Many Masters have spoken about its effectiveness and power which is unmatched beyond doubt. The great master Adi Shankaracharya put it very eloquently and very effectively when he said,

> *'satsangatve nissangatvam (satsanga gives rise to non-attachment)*
> *nissangatve nirmohatvam (non-attachment leads to freedom from delusion)*
> *nirmohatve nischalatattvam (freedom from delusion leads to steadfastness)*
> *nischalatattve jeevanmuktih' (steadfastness gives rise to liberation)*

What is this Truth or *Sat* that our *Rishis* speak about when they say '*Sat Chit Ananda*' or when they say '*Satsanga*'?

They said:
-*Truth is that which is permanent*
-*Truth is that which is not subject to change, it is changeless*
-*Truth is that which is not subject to death, disease, or decay*
-*Truth means that what was yesterday, what is today and what shall be in future*

Sat is the existential truth. Right from the time existence came into being and up to this present moment it has not changed. It remains eternal. It is the *Atman* or the *Brahman* which is constant. It is that which has been, is and shall always remain; it is that Consciousness. That is the truth we are seeking as the goal of our life. That truth is within us as the eternal witness, which is unaffected and unchanged. That is the truth spoken in *Satsanga*. So, we are engaged in the company of those people who are seeking that very same truth. We continue to explore that truth which is the Divinity - that changeless reality inside us.

Wherever this truth is discussed, where there is a *Guru* who's talking about it, where there are others who are seeking this truth earnestly, all such gatherings are called *Satsanga*. Adi Shankaracharya has said '*Satsangatve nissangatvam*'; *Satsanga* leads to *Nissangatvam*. *Nissangatvam* means non-attachment or detachment. When we constantly keep hearing the truth again and again, it serves as a reminder to us. We humans are in dire need of such constant reminders. In this world, we are constantly focused on what is happening outside of us and, therefore, our mind has been deeply conditioned into a reality which is transient and impermanent but appears as real. Thus, a constant reminder helps us to start un-conditioning ourselves and removing the preconceived notions that we carry so strongly in our mind.

Even on social media, when we listen to various Masters and see their videos, what are we doing? We are constantly reinforcing in our mind and reminding ourselves of the truth. We are surrounding ourselves with the truth all the time and, slowly, the mind starts to accept it and become detached from this world which we have been so engrossed and attached to and which we have been thinking of as real.

One of the most important prayers for the seekers on this path is '*Asato Ma Sad Gamaya...*' We pray to Lord Almighty, the Universal Consciousness, to lead us from the unreal, transient and temporary world to which we are bound and attached to the real world within us which is changeless and constant. We are currently engrossed in this unreal world, mistaking it to be real, so we pray to be led to the truth and the constant reality which is ever present within us.

Even for our *Satsanga,* this prayer is a reminder that helps us to detach from this world which is full of sorrow, likes and dislikes, good and bad. As we become established, we no longer like all those attractions of the world which were pulling us; rather, we begin enjoying our silence. We like to be ourselves, by ourselves and slowly move away from the outer noises into our inner silence. That means we are becoming non-attached. So, '*Satsangatve Nissangatvam.*'

Next is '*Nissangatve Nirmohatvam*'. What does this detachment do to us? It leads us to the removal of the delusion in our mind. We then consider the outer world, the world of all these attractions, to be 'not real'. We are able to see things in a different perspective. We slowly develop discrimination, by which we are able to differentiate between the permanent and the impermanent. Consequently, we start to question whatever is impermanent, because we need to make choices for our chosen goal of life.

We all are allotted a certain time on Earth, the duration of which we are not aware of. Definitely, it is limited and so the choices we make are very important. We must be clear as to where we must invest our time, energy, and efforts. As seekers, we must question ourselves whether we are investing more time in the world which is temporary and constantly changing, where at every corner lies a possible discomfort or unhappiness, or whether we are trying to make the effort which is going to give us a permanent state of bliss or happiness. We start to discriminate between the real and the unreal, the permanent and the impermanent, and this comes only when we get to the point of *Nirmohatvam* (*Nir* – without; *moha* – attachment). We start moving away from those things which attract and lure us. The delusion starts to melt away.

Where does freedom from delusion lead us to? *'Nirmohatve Nischalatattvam'* - *Nirmohatve* leads us to *Nischaltattvam.* Once the veil between the real and the unreal is removed, we become equanimous, steady. We are no longer impacted by the sorrows of the world nor attracted to the joys of the world. We become equal minded and wise (*Stithprajna*). We become steady; we develop fortitude. We operate in the world without getting either agitated or excited, and that is called *Sambhava (equal-mindedness)*.

It is this equal mindedness (*Nischalatattve*) that leads us to liberation, *'Nischalatattve Jeevanmuktih'*. It is in the state of equal mindedness that the witness awakens within us. This witness within is able to see everything as a play, as an illusion. It knows everything is unreal. It looks at life as a game, a drama or a movie; and that is when we get liberated. What is this liberation? Liberation is not that we die, it is not that we leave the body. Liberation is that this mind no longer has any power over us; we are no longer reacting to any of the attractions and repulsions of this world and we are now free.

Only the mind comes in the way of experiencing our reality. It creates delusions, desires and attachments, due to which we fail to recognise the reality. If as sincere seekers we invest our time, energy and efforts with full faith and dedication, then surely at the end of these forty days we will be liberated from the clutches of the mind. It is *Satsanga*, the company of the seekers of truth, the company of teachers of truth, which will help us to make this journey of Self-Realisation, break the bond of the mind and start experiencing the immortal truth of the Self. Such is the importance of *Satsanga*.

Our *Sanatana Dharma* (Eternal Principle) holds the

Parampara (tradition) of bringing this eternal, immortal knowledge of the Self from the Master to those who are seeking it. This knowledge, this wisdom, flows from one to the other and, as more and more lamps get lit with this wisdom, with this knowledge, each lamp in turn starts to light many more lamps. This is the *Mahima* (greatness) of *Satsanga*.

Gurukulas (residential schools of holistic education) of ancient India were established by sages and seers on the principle of *Satsanga*. The *Guru* (teacher) and the disciples used to live together to have this experiential process of learning. They used to be constantly engaged in dialogue, discussion and practises until the knowledge gained became a way of life for each one. The students never left the *Gurukula* for their homes, not even for short breaks. They stayed in the *Gurukula* in the presence of the Master for the entire 10-12 years of their education, until they became virtuous embodiments of the truth and immersed in that oneness. Such was the powerful effect of *Satsanga* in *Gurukulas*.

Useful Tips

Take down notes and start reflecting upon what has been discussed in these chapters. Ruminate about it, reflect about it, and then marinate yourself in those thoughts. To marinate means to remain in those thoughts for the whole day. A change will begin to take place. It will reflect as the beginning of a transformation in your own perspective. These methods have been given by the seers and our ancestors since ancient times and yield valid results.

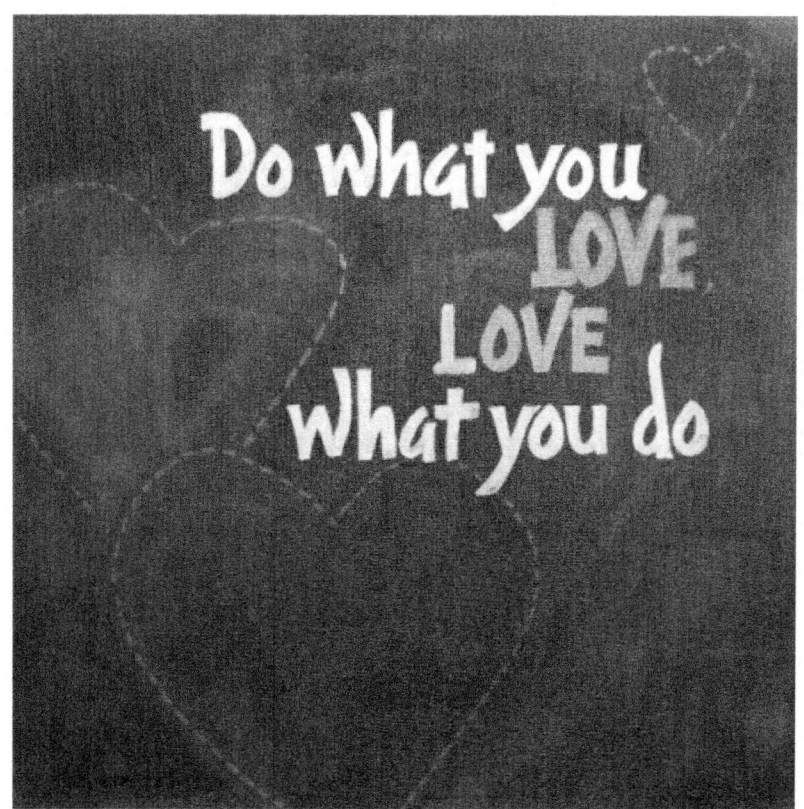

CHAPTER 7: TRIKARANSHUDDHI

In the olden times Kings like Janaka, who was himself a realised soul, would honour all saints and sages who would come in their court and engage in *Satsanga* (company of seekers and knowers of truth). That was Janaka's favourite pastime, his favourite way of keeping himself surrounded by the light of wisdom. We too have been fortunate in our life to have received this wisdom from our Master and from many other Masters as well, because we have remained open in our pursuit in the journey of realising the truth of our being.

One of the guiding principles of this experiential journey of Self-realisation is called *Trikaranshuddhi.* '*Tri*' means three. '*Karan*' means that there are three aspects of thought, word and action. '*Shuddhi*' means purity, making our thoughts, our words (which is what we speak and what we write) and our actions pure.

Why is *Trikaranshuddhi* so relevant in experiencing the truth of ourselves? When we look at truth, as discussed in earlier Chapters, the truth of the Self is the Higher Consciousness (Divine Consciousness) which is permanent and changeless. But, at a transactional level, how do we live this truth? What is the truth that is guiding us at all times? That truth is when we are able to align what we are thinking to what we are saying and what we are saying to what we do in life. It means there is no gap between what we are thinking, what we are saying and what we are doing. So, we mean what we say and what we say is what we do. Incidentally, that is also the definition of INTEGRITY – that there is no gap between the thoughts that are arising in our mind and what we are subsequently doing with those thoughts.

Today, everywhere in the world, there seems to be a disconnect between thoughts, words, and actions. That is indeed the reason why the world is going through a period of turmoil, destruction and dissolution. It's because all linkages between thoughts, words and actions have been removed. There is a huge gap between what the world is thinking, what the world is saying and what the world is doing. By definition, when there is a gap between the three, that is called FALSITY. The opposite of truth is falseness. We are living in a false world, a world where everything is being presented in such a way that we can influence others without ever meaning what we are saying. Also, there is a huge moral bankruptcy of character. However, we are all in search of experiencing the truth, for which we need to rise above falsity.

When we talk of the Master's message or about the goal of life, what is the best way of putting that into practice? Once we have done the three stages of experiential learning of *Shravana, Manana*, and *Nididhyasana*, that is, listening, contemplating, inquiring about the teachings and removing our doubts, then the last stage is *Nididhyasana,* where we practice and implement them in our life, so that they become a way of being.

Now, we need to know the effective way of *Nididhyasana* so that we may rightly integrate our learning into our life and become one with it. We all know that everything starts with a thought and we know the power of thought. Upanishads extol this power by giving the principle of '*Yad Bhavam, Tad Bhavati'.* Let us first understand the meaning of *Bhavam* and *Bhavati. Bhavam* is the sum total of a thought and the intensity of one's feeling or emotion attached to that thought. *Bhavati* means to come to pass, to happen. So, the Upanishadic principle '*Yad Bhavam, Tad Bhavati'* connotes that whatever a human being strongly thinks about, feels for and emotes about, he or she starts to attract that in his or her life. This is clearly noticed in our daily lives. When we desire something, a thought comes to us and, if we really pine for it, we start to take steps to acquire it.

As seekers, our whole journey of experiencing the Divine

Consciousness starts with the thought 'I am Divine, I am God, I am pure Consciousness, I am the Truth that I am seeking'. When this thought couples with the intensity of seeking, it starts to create a power that is unstoppable. And this thought, if it is expressed by us in language, either through spoken words or in writing, starts to acquire a strength of its own. This is because the feeling of intensity, the *Bhava* in the thought, now gets expressed either as the spoken word or the written word.

Now, one would say, 'How can a feeling or emotion be expressed in writing?'. Well, during our lives we have read books by many authors. There are some books that appeal to us instantly and we connect with them, whereas there are some other books that we just want to put down the minute we start reading them. What's the difference between the two writers? Why does a certain book or a certain writing appeal to us while other writings do not? It's because the emotions and the energy of the writer (author) also gets communicated through the written word.

For those of you who are new, I have a blog site called 'I am I - Love Light and Joy' on WordPress. When I started to write my blogs six years ago, many people would tell me that, when they read them, they experienced an energy coming through those words, they experienced a power in those words. I had the same direct experience while reading the messages of my Master and of some other Gurus. I have experienced the same feedback from others when they read my writings. Therefore, that *Bhava* which comes through the intensity of the thought also manifests itself through words, through language.

Once we connect that language to our daily actions and we ensure that there is no gap between what we have thought and what we have expressed, and what we have expressed is what we are going to put in action, then we are living a life of truth. We are living a life of honesty, of doing what we truly believe in. And what we truly believe in is what we start manifesting in our life.

Unlike politicians, we don't think about something, say something else and then do a completely different thing. For us, there is integrity, and this is what builds our habits and our character. Ultimately, it all starts with the thought. The power of that one little tiny thought, if invested with the energy of emotion, of feeling, of intensity, suddenly manifests itself as powerful words. These words have the ability to change, to influence and to inspire others. They have the ability to touch the chords which are deep within each one of us.

Nevertheless, this ability will come only when there is an integrity between thoughts and words; when the thought comes from the source of Consciousness and we are not doing any addition or dilution to the original thought or energy that is coming in. We are all carriers of that energy. As long as we are pure vessels, which means that there is no adulteration or contamination in our thoughts, in our speech and in our actions, that starts to express itself as AUTHENTICITY and we start living an authentic life. Then, whoever comes in touch with us starts to experience that authenticity first hand.

When we meet people, we are able to immediately recognise the difference between an authentic person and a person who is faking. It's almost as simple as reading a book. To some, the energy speaks; to some, the arrogance speaks; to some, the humility speaks; to some, the very power of the words and the effect that those words have on our heart and on our mind speaks. Being authentic is extremely important in this journey of Self-Realisation, in this journey of experiencing the truth of our being and of practicing this truth.

In Hanuman Chalisa, Tulasi Das ji talks about this *Trikaranshuddhi* where he says, '*Man Kram Vachan Dhyan Jo Laye*' - that Hanuman's quality is that he is able to align his thoughts, his words and his actions. This indicates a life of truth, of purity, of integrity.

So, we know that the whole cycle of habits, of character, starts from a mere thought. This means that thought is not so powerless, and if we bring in the right thought then we can achieve the right results. What is the right thought that we are now introducing as we go into the practice phase of our journey of experiencing Self-realisation? We are bringing in the thought that 'I am Divine'. And this thought has to be completely communicated in our heart, mind and soul.

Language is very powerful, so we should be very careful with the words that we choose. Whichever words we use, they start to manifest. Therefore, all negative words should be removed from our life because, when we say 'I cannot', then it 'shall not' happen. If we say 'I can, I will, I must', then it shall happen. We must replace all negative words with positive words and, once we become careful, we are alert about it and it becomes a part of our awareness, then suddenly we understand that the power of creation lies within each one of us.

For us, the crucial checkpoint for manifestation lies where we start the thinking process. We should be alert and check ourselves regarding the thought which we are bringing:

- Is it in line with my truth, my Divinity?
- Is it pure?
- Is it positive?

If it is, we will see how quickly the experiences of our truth start coming to us. This is because now we are programming every cell in our body. We are programming our nervous system because that is where the mind starts to create the thought. So, at that time of programming the thought, we are adding to it the emotion, the integrity; and we are synchronizing it into our thought. Then, it comes to our tongue and, through our organs of action (our hands, our limbs), the whole thought starts to travel through every cell of our body.

Because the command is uniform there is an alignment, there is no disconnection, we start becoming aligned to what the thought is.

So, the power of creation lies in the thought. This is also how the universe was created. The Universal Consciousness wanted to create a world which it could enjoy. Therefore, from that thought creation was made. That is how all of nature came in and that is how various beings came in, because it all came from a thought in the attribute-less Consciousness.

It all starts at the point of thought. So, if we start practising the alignment of our thoughts, words and actions, we can begin to work on the purity of those thoughts. How will this purity come? Through *Satsanga* (company of seekers or knowers of truth), through constant reminder. For example, we can keep away from all negative influences and information that comes to us through social media and from all the negativity that surrounds us.

Through *Satsanga*, we start to go through an intense phase of detaching from the world. Because the world is so full of negativity, we start to shy away from it, we go into our own cocoon, we start to withdraw like a tortoise. We withdraw inside ourselves because that is the phase of purification, that is the phase of *Parayanam* (intense devotion towards self-transformation). It is a phase when we say 'no' to the negative world and surround ourselves with the message of the truth. We repeatedly remind ourselves that 'I am not this body; I am that Divine Consciousness.' And when we marinate in this thought, our thoughts start to alter. The command that these thoughts start to give us is very different. So, we have to start correcting the feeder which is feeding these thoughts inside of us. We have to start creating a positive flow of thoughts in our mind. And that's where this correction course starts to happen for us and we start moving towards experiencing our Self.

Useful tip

If, for the rest of the day and tomorrow, we can consciously start focusing on aligning our thoughts to our words and our words to our actions, and start focusing on improving the quality of our thoughts, then we will begin to get an experience. And, as we have been noting down all our experiences in our journal, we will start to see that there is a shift which is beginning to come through this practice.

CHAPTER 8: LAW OF KARMA

We have taken this 40-day vow of self-transformation to experience the presence of the Divine consciousness or the Atman, as our scriptures call it. Therefore, we are focusing completely on our inner journey and how the inner journey is actually manifested in the external world. We have spoken about *Trikaranshuddhi*, the purity and the unity of thought, word and action. Everything in our life starts from our thoughts; and those thoughts manifest into our actions, which lead to our habits, which in turn lead to building our character.

Now, we will take a step further to understand one of the principal laws that govern life on this planet. It is important for us to understand the operating framework within which we are all experiencing this world. First, we must understand what this *Jagat* (world) is and how it operates. Then, we will be able to understand our relationship with it. This will help us to carve out a path for ourselves, so that we can experience that supreme oneness which is the goal of our life as well as of this book.

I am sure everybody knows about the Law of *Karma* (action). Simply put, the Law of *Karma* states that every action has a result. For every action, there is a preceding cause. That cause leads to action, every action leads to a result and that result becomes the cause of another action. That is how we remain in the loop of action, reaction and interaction. That's how our life goes on. Be it in our personal, private world or be it in the material world outside, this is the principle at play everywhere. This is how science has progressed, this is how man has progressed and this is how the whole universe is supported by this law of action, result and consequence. It can be known as the law of cause and effect.

It is important to note that the cause of action lies in

the thought. It is this that forms the basis of the action and gives birth to it. It makes us perform an action which, as a natural consequence, will have a reaction, thereby perpetuating a continuum of life.

Karma is also the basis of another law, the Law of Reincarnation. If we perform a good action, there is a good result which goes into a kind of Bank where all our good actions are accumulated. However, if there are some actions which are not so good, they act as a withdrawal from that Bank. It is said that good actions are like an asset and bad actions are like a liability on our personal balance sheet of *Karma*. But, the good actions and the bad actions do not net-off. This means that we have to experience the results of all our good actions as well as all our bad actions.

We would be focussing on dealing with the present lifetime rather than on our past lives. However, we do understand that there is a law of reincarnation, that there is a past life, because each one is born in a different country, in a different environment, in different circumstances. Some are born with healthy bodies and some are born with deformities. Some live for a few months, some live for a hundred years. Some are born in countries which are so prosperous that they have never seen poverty, and some are born in poverty-stricken countries that have never seen good times. If there was no law of *Karma* or reincarnation, then one cannot explain how people take birth in either very adverse or very opulent circumstances.

There must be something which causes this unequal distribution of health, wealth, prosperity and understanding. Some children are born very smart and quickly pick up the thread of science. Some pick up on spirituality and there are some who go through life very slowly. So, there must be a cause for these unequal roles on this planet. *Sanathana Dharma* (Eternal Principle) explains it through the law of *Karma*. However, now we are going to focus on this lifetime, on what is in our hands to control.

When we talk of *Moksha* (liberation) and Self-realisation as our goal, the whole idea is to get away from the accumulated balance of *Karma* that we are carrying. How do we make this *Karma*, these positive and negative balances that we are carrying, inoperable? There must be some precipitating cause which made each one of us take birth now. There must be something that still needs to be exhausted. Many people explain our tendencies and reactions through these *Prarabdha Karmas* (accumulated effects of past lives that impact this lifetime) which we have come to address in this lifetime. Essentially, like Newton's law, for every action there is a reaction, and we can see the result. If we speak angrily, the result is a fight. If we speak lovingly, it results in service and selflessness. If we work hard, we get a promotion. If we are negligent, we are penalised, and so on. That's how nature has been structured.

Let us clarify our understanding on finding a permanent exit mode from bondage on earth. Be aware and clear that everything is in our hands. It is our thoughts that lead to the words or language which we speak or express. What we express then becomes our actions. Therefore, everything that happens in our life is a result of our thoughts. However, this does not mean that we are helpless or controlled by our thoughts; we humans have the ability to control our thoughts and we are empowered to do so. If we use this ability to rectify our thoughts we can ensure that our actions bring us positive or good *Karma*. However, our ultimate aim is to not accrue any good or bad *Karma* in this lifetime; freedom from the *Karmic* cycle. This aspect will be dealt with in detail in the forthcoming days and we will be practising this way of life through this *Parayanam*.

Much gratitude to the Divine Consciousness and everyone on this journey of Self-realisation.

CHAPTER 9: LAW OF CREATIVE LIFE FORCE

We are going to systematically progress by understanding the laws and mechanics, and all that it takes to fathom what life is all about and who we are, so as to experience the truth of ourselves. One by one, we are going to lift the layers of all that we have never been able to fully penetrate. So, today on day 9, we will talk about another beautiful law that governs this universe and, in fact, the entire creation.

It is the law of the Creative Life Force. It is also referred to as the principle of EFV- Energy, Frequency and Vibration. Everything that we see, hear, touch and smell; everything that we do not see, smell, touch, fathom, or experience; all that is sentient and insentient; all that is on this planet and on all other planets in our galaxy and beyond is nothing but a manifestation of energy. Everything that has life has energy in it. Even everything that is stationary and so-called non-living also has energy. The energy may not be in a state of movement, it could be as blocked energy or inert energy. Whatever be the case, the fact is that everything has been created out of energy.

The life force which is inside us and the life force that is in a plant or an animal is one and the same. It is the same energetic principle. All the energy which is around us and inside of us has a certain frequency and a certain vibration. Every being operates at a different level of frequency and vibration. Among human beings, there are some who operate on a higher frequency and vibration. These are the enlightened ones, the saints and sages, who are able to manifest, out of thin air, whatever their consciousness desires.

Outer energy is the level where science has reached, but

the power of creation which is inside of us, which we call as God, has not been understood. Because of lack of evidence, science argues with spirituality. There are some things which we don't know and don't understand, and that which we don't know and don't understand we often end up debating and arguing about. Nevertheless, our forefathers, our ancient seers and our sages not only understood these things but also experienced them. Therefore, they created a methodology for us to experience them too.

It is said that 'What can be experienced, cannot necessarily be expressed.' So the scientists have not been able to put it into a theory or a law and publish papers about it. Soon, the time is coming when this energy will reveal itself. We have already reached the God particle so, in the next 8 to 10 years, all that seemed impossible and that we did not understand will get revealed, because the time of revelation has arrived. The principle has always been there. It is not that something new is going to happen to us or that we are going to perceive something new. We have always perceived it, but we have not understood it.

Enlightenment can come in an instant. In a moment, we can experience that which we have been seeking ever since we took human birth. As it comes in a moment, it is quite digital in nature, like the binary system of zero and one. It is either there or it is not there. So, whatever we experience in this life and perhaps also experienced in previous lifetimes is nothing but the continuation of our preparation to move into a higher frequency and vibration that will enable us to receive the frequency of the Universal Consciousness, the Energetic Source.

When the concept of God arises, we all agree that it is a Higher Being. We all have different ways of relating to that Being, we all have different religions that talk about the same Being called the Creator or God. He can manifest anything, He can manifest our desires and He can manifest objects and can listen to and answer our prayers.

We have tried to describe that ever-present Consciousness or God through three distinguishable qualities and characteristics. We say God is omnipresent, omniscient and omnipotent. When we say that God is omnipresent, we mean that God is present everywhere at all times, no matter which country we live in, no matter the physical distances, no matter the religion we follow and the language we speak.

This God is not only omnipresent but also omniscient, which means that He is all knowing. He is able to listen and eavesdrop on all our conversations and even know our thoughts.

God is also omnipotent, which means He is all powerful. He can manifest, create and do anything at will. Nevertheless, we cannot see Him. This Being, which is present everywhere and has all the knowledge and power, can only be experienced in the form of energy, and we know that everything is energy.

The reason we are breathing and our body is functioning is because there is energy in it. When that energetic principle leaves us, the body stops breathing and the heart stops beating. So, there is energy within us and there is energy around us. It is that energy around us which science has constantly been trying to tap into. Much advancement has been made regarding the Energy, Frequency and Vibration (EFV) of the energy that exists outside of us. Whatever technological advancements we see are based on what scientists have been able to do with this outer energy. Nevertheless, they have not been able to experience, understand and express the energy which is inside of us.

We are talking about this because our goal is to experience the Divine Consciousness inside each one of us. Whatever principle is outside, that same principle is inside of us. So, we should know what Divine consciousness means to us. Are we looking for a person, or an entity or an energetic presence within? We started on this journey of 40 days in order to experience this energetic principle which is inside of us, which has always been within us through every birth that we have taken. It's just that we have been ignorant about this principle. Though we are quite smart about what happens in the outside world and like to comment about it, it is this Divinity, this Higher Consciousness, that we actually want to experience.

As we wake up from our ignorance, as we start becoming aware and experiencing this Consciousness, it is imperative that our energy will rise. The frequency at which this energy will vibrate will keep going higher and higher. Our bodies are being readied for this. We have a vessel (body), and that vessel has a certain capacity which is being upgraded slowly. Our ability to hold that energy is being improved and increased gradually. Otherwise, we would not be able to withstand its immense intensity if it were to come to us suddenly.

Last night we had a meditation and healing was experienced. Many have started to receive this healing energy. What is this healing energy? Why and how can it travel? When this group representing several different continents meditates, instantly, we direct this energy everywhere. Our scientists may ask 'How is that possible? How can you direct this energy at will by focussing? And how can this energy be perceived by others?' It is something that you have to experience in order to understand how it happens. We cannot debate or argue about this energy, but once we receive and experience it, we can draw our own conclusions. We all are trying to come to grips with this higher energy and, once we reach that steady state of consciousness where energy is constantly flowing through us, we will feel bliss.

When we are blissed out, we are not concerned about what is happening outside because we have had a direct experience. What is happening in the world outside is nothing but the reaction, reflection and resound of our inner Self. If we are confused, fearful, argumentative or angry, then that is what we will receive back from the world. It is the energy principle -

Whatever energy we give is the energy we receive back. That is how this energy operates. The whole of this universe which we call *Maya* (illusion) is nothing but the experience that we are receiving. It is what we are projecting is what is coming back to us.

I will share a small experience that I had many years ago. My Master Bhagawan Sri Sathya Sai Baba came to me in one of my meditations, and I asked Him, 'How is it that You are unaffected by all that goes on in this world?'. He said, 'Do you want to experience how I remain unaffected?'. I answered, 'Yes'. He said, 'Come with me', and took me to a place where there was absolute silence. My mind was completely still. We soon reached a place where there was a beautiful chair which was all lit up, which had a radiance and a glow of its own. He said, 'Come', and went and sat on it. Then, he just extended His right hand outwards and another smaller chair manifested next to His. He asked me to sit down. So, I sat there and remained absolutely still. When I looked to the front, I saw that there was a white screen, about five or six metres high, that just went on for the entire length of the horizon. As far as I could see, there was just this big white screen. I was wondering what it was when, suddenly, I realised that there were some thoughts coming into my mind. As I was experiencing them, I saw they were being projected on that big screen. Whatever I was thinking was actually getting projected, and Baba could see everything that was going on in my mind. I tried hard to control my thoughts, but the more I tried the more thoughts came. That's how the mind works. You try to stop the mind and it starts to play with you. I could see my Master just smiling and watching. He looked at me and I said, 'Oh, now I see how You are able to read what is going on in my mind'. He smiled. I asked, 'How come You are not getting disturbed by it?'. He answered, 'It is a show going on and I am just watching. I am just a witness'. Then I saw some people walking towards us. They were not aware of our presence. Whatever was happening between them (verbally as well at the thought level) was also being projected on the white screen, which started to get full. Many thoughts were overlapping, and some were in conflict with others. I realised that the conflicting thoughts were causing challenges and creating actions. Some people were getting angry, some were happy and some were receiving love. My Master, who was watching everything, said, 'If you want to enjoy this, you can also sit like Me and watch everything'.

Thus, He made me understand two things: that *Karma* (action-consequence) starts from thoughts and, since there are billions of us and our thoughts are not always pure and selfless, they can be in conflict with the needs of others because all of us are obsessed with 'me, my family and my needs'. All the *Karma* and all the upheaval that we see in the world starts with a thought. I realised that the entity called God or the Divine Master was doing nothing to create *Karma*. It was just a mere witness to what was going on. He advised me saying that to be a mere witness, I just had to go and sit next to Him, implying that I had to become thoughtless. As soon as my thoughts stopped, I stopped projecting onto the screen and, since I did not have any projections on the universal screen of *Karma*, there was no other thought that was conflicting. Thus, I was taught this very beautiful principle of how life operates.

As discussed in the previous chapter, our thoughts have energy. Intensity of thought means that we are putting energy into our thoughts. *Bhava* (feeling) is the energy associated with thought. And, when a thought gets energy, it becomes like an arrow which has to go and hit its target and therefore the thought manifests. This is the creative energetic principle that has created the whole world. This is how everything came into being, including us. This is how we can not only experience our own energy, but also tap into everybody's energy, since there is no two energies, there is only one energy.

In yesterday's meditation, I said there was a ring of white

light with which everybody was joined. Many may have thought that I was just using imaginary words, but a ring of light actually gets formed. In fact, that light is everywhere. Once we are able to connect on the same frequency and vibration, we are able to connect to that one common life force which is present in all of us. It is important to understand the principle behind it so as to understand the experiences when they come.

We will go deeper and deeper into this understanding to know that, when we say that there is God inside of us, there is a Divinity inside of us, there is Consciousness inside of us, it is nothing but an energetic presence. In the beginning, when that presence gets revealed to us, it is uncomfortable. Some call it *Kundalini Shakti*, the serpent power which is coiled up in the *Muladhara Chakra* (Root Chakra/ Base energy centre in the human body) and slowly starts to rise and move through the other *Chakras* (energy centres). The *Muladhara* or base *Chakra* is where Ganesha is present. He is the protector of this energy. From there, he hands over this energy to the *Swadhisthana Chakra* (Sacral Chakra), where Mother Durga is present. She is the Creative life force. The whole of creation has been manifested by the Mother, by mother Nature. Then, the Mother rises with this energy until it reaches the third eye, where the third eye of Shiva brings it into alignment and moves to the *Sahasrara Chakra* (Crown Chakra) which is the Formless Consciousness principle or the Shiva principle. Here the union of Shakti and Shiva takes place.

Many of you would have been experiencing this intense energy in the *Sahasrara Chakra*. During all my waking time and in my sleep, my head is pulsating with energy. Sometimes it is so strong that I feel my whole body is jerking, because now the energy is moving very rapidly. This is true for all of us and it is also true for animals and plants. There are some very beautiful souls in our group who can communicate with animals, and also others who are able to communicate with plants. This communication happens through the one common energetic life principle.

This is what I had to share with you today about the journey of experiencing that one Consciousness. This is coming from the source of Consciousness. It is ONE not TWO. Some of you may not believe my words, some of you may think, 'Let's see where this craziness takes us to'. I can only tell that everything that is going to happen to you during these 40 days entirely depends upon you and you alone. It is important to seek it intensely and to have complete surrender and belief, without any kind of barrier or doubt in the mind.

CHAPTER 10: LAW OF OPPOSING FORCES

We have spoken about energy, frequency and vibration, which is the law of the Creative Life Force and, before that, we spoke about the Law of *Karma*, of cause and effect. In continuation with that understanding of the energetic principle, which is life within and without, we will now talk about another principle or law called the Law of Opposing Forces. We may also call it the Law of Duality.

What do I mean by opposing forces and Duality? We are discussing this in order to understand the framework which regulates life on this planet and the laws that impact that life. Such understanding will give us a clear cognizance of what this creation is and who we are with reference to this creation.

This reference point is important. It's like those basic things that we learnt in school. It's what we need to understand when we are journeying towards experiencing the Self; how we are related to everything else and how this Oneness or this one Consciousness is everywhere, despite the fact that everything looks so different. We are all different in our looks, in our thinking, in the food we eat, in our language. Therefore, there is duality everywhere, which means that there is much choice, variation, and diversity. Everything in this world has been put in two diametrically opposite forces. I call it the Law of Opposing Forces.

So, what is this law? It is the law which says there is darkness and light, good and evil, right and wrong, night and day. Wherever we look, we find this law in operation. Actually, this play is very important for the drama of life to take place. It is very critical for us to experience the truth of ourselves.

It is the playing field into which each individual soul, carrying the same Consciousness as the universal energetic life force, is born. The soul starts to separate itself from the mothership or the universal life force which is present everywhere and comes down and takes a body. Since it has a body, it has a name, religion, culture etc., so it starts to see itself as separate. This is how the whole world of duality starts to take shape as soon as we are born on this planet.

At birth, we are given a name and we start to see ourselves as either a son or a daughter in a family. We are told that we are a family and that this family is separate from other families. We go to school, sit in a class and see ourselves as separate from other students. As we keep growing, this separation and duality continues taking place. We keep separating ourselves from everything else because that's our whole sense of self identity. We just keep seeing separation, separation and separation everywhere. When we see goodness, we start to gravitate towards it. When we see what we don't like, we start to move away from it. These dual forces of good and bad, light and dark, keep operating the entire play of Consciousness.

Now, if we are divine beings and if there's one energetic Consciousness, we could ask why negativity or darkness was ever created. If all is the same Consciousness, why is there a separation between good and bad? It's a very logical question and each one of us should definitely put some attention and time to investigate that. Why is there a play and why is this play so important? Our investigation will tell us that this play will continue till perpetuity because it is what life on this planet is about. It plays between two extreme polarities, and we come between these two. We have to find our way between two reference points; one is the extreme limit of right and the other is the extreme limit of wrong. In between, the whole play of life takes place. All situations, events, and circumstances of life take place between these polarities. We grow up from childhood into youth, into adulthood, into old age and we die. This entire drama happens within the playfield of opposing forces.

Why is this duality essential and how does it help us to experience the truth of our innate Divine Consciousness? We know that, in order to make butter, the milk must be churned. We have to apply another force to separate the cream from the milk. One may say that we are hurting the milk because we are applying force on it. When we make butter out of that cream, we again apply some force to create butter. In the case of carbon, an opposite force must be applied to it in order to create a diamond. When we apply an opposing force which is not inherent in the essential element of an object, a new form is created. It brings new qualities which we consider far more attractive and precious.

We love daytime because there is night. How hard it would be for us to live in one of those Nordic countries where there is night for three or four months, and then daytime for a couple of months! We appreciate goodness only because there are some people who are not so good. We appreciate light because there is darkness. Negativity inspires us to become positive. If we look back at our lives, we will see that every time adverse circumstances came, we rose to the challenges and became better versions of ourselves. We thought that all those challenges were insurmountable, but look how we overcame them! We became wiser, maybe not stronger in the body, but stronger in spirit. All those situations and events came into our life for a certain reason and were orchestrated by the Divine Consciousness, which is as much inside of us as outside of us.

Everybody who comes into our life comes for a certain reason. That reason is to make us grow and evolve into a better version of ourselves. All our relationships, be it our partners, our children, our employees, our friends or any other relationships are geared towards this singular goal of self-improvement.

Every situation takes us a little further forward, a little closer to who we truly are, because life is a progression, not a regression. Just as we progress in our careers, we progress in our life to achieve our real goal of experiencing that Consciousness which is inside of us, of knowing who we truly are. The so-called negativity or darkness has actually been very beautifully created by the Almighty Consciousness only for us to accept it, face it and grow from it. As we learn the instincts of how to overcome that opposing force, we grow.

There is a beautiful example about a child who one day came home from school carrying a small glass bowl filled with water. In it, there was a tiny tadpole and, in the centre of the bowl, there was a small rock. The mother asked her son, 'What is this?' The child replied, 'We had a science class, and the teacher told us to take this bowl home and keep watching the tadpole every day, keeping an eye on what is happening'. So, every day, the child would keep looking at the bowl for hours. He would watch the little tiny tadpole swimming around and trying to climb onto the rock, without success. It would slip and fall back into the water, but it would not give up. The same routine of the tadpole slipping down went on for weeks. One day, the child went running to the mother and exclaimed, 'Oh Mom, come, come, see what's happened!' Now, the tadpole was actually sitting on top of the rock. The child was very excited and reported the news to the science teacher. She asked the student, 'So tell me what do you think happened?' Not understanding, the boy said, 'I just know that I am so happy and excited that the tadpole is sitting on the rock!' Then, the science teacher explained, 'Look, every time the tadpole was trying to climb the rock, it would slip and fall back because its legs were not strong enough. But, over the days, as it kept trying, its legs muscles got gradually stronger and one day it could push itself onto the rock'.

In the same way, for each one of us as we have been facing obstacles and challenging situations in our lives, unknown to us there were some muscles inside of us- spiritual muscles or the muscles of the spirit or of the creative life force within- which started getting stronger and slowly took us up to this point where we are attending this *Satsanga* (gathering of seekers and knowers of Truth of one's Self) today. This is the importance of the so-called opposing forces in our life. Without them, we would never progress. Without challenges, man would not have advanced in science and technology. That is how we have grown and that is how this game of life is played. That is the reason why all these opposing forces are right now present in the entire world and the entire world is going through a phase of deconstruction

It is said that the 'Old order will go away and the new will come.' We observe that the whole universe is realigning itself. The old and the new cannot coexist. Only when the old crumbles, the new comes in. We cannot make a new house on top of an old one; we must pull down the old one so that the new one can be built. That is how we have constantly recreated, reformed ourselves and evolved, becoming better and better. Recollect those days when something unfavourable happened, or things did not go as we had planned, how angry and upset we used to get. Perhaps today we don't lose our temper or, out of 100 times, we now lose it two or three times. All of us, no matter where we are, have been growing; and this growth always comes when we face a challenge. The challenge tests us, pushes us, goads us, makes us better than who we believe we are. That is the role of the so-called negativity.

Each one of us on this planet is the manifestation of the same Divine life force, and this was true for Rama and Ravana as well. Both were the embodiments of the same Divine Consciousness. Both were playing a role; one used it in a positive context and the other in a negative context. Both these contexts are relevant for us only to give us an understanding of who we are and what is our reference point. Are we on the right, on the left or in the centre?

We all need references; we all need an understanding of what's going on and why. We need to understand that everything is a reflection of our inner feelings. If our inner understanding changes, everything around us starts to shift. To reach that point, we need something to push us and edge us forward. As soon as we think we have evolved and we have reached somewhere, there is always a test round the corner for us to check how far we have moved forward in our understanding. That is the Consciousness checking whether our change is permanent or temporary. Have we really grown and moved or are we still at the threshold? That is how we have been becoming better and better at dealing with life and its situations.

So, this whole play of light and dark is only designed for us to experience that one Consciousness. The so-called duality in life, the so-called multiplicity in life is nothing but a reflection of that same one Consciousness. Every person that comes into our life brings us all the experiences we need. They are only trying to push us so that we can see that one energetic Consciousness which is within and without, which pervades everywhere and everything. That is why this play of two forces continues to happen and will continue till there is life on this planet. This is the way this drama happens; this is how the framework has been set in life. But in our ignorance of it, we get serious, we start judging, we start calling names, we start blaming people and thus get caught into what we call *Maya* (illusion).

If we understand the permanence and the impermanence, the Reality and *Maya,* we will be able to understand the framework of life, who we truly are, and therefore live life as Divinity - *Sat Chit Ananda* (bliss that results from the awareness of the existential truth).

Atma Shatakam or *Nirvana Shatakam,* by Adi

Shankaracharya, exhorts us to realise that the goal of life is *Sat Chit Ananda*, which is without attributes, qualities or form. However, to reach that state of *Sat Chit Ananda*, we have to go beyond right and wrong, good and bad, likes and dislikes. We have to go beyond the idea of being in a sacred place or an unholy place, beyond any particular association that we may have carried about ourselves so far.

We reach a point where we understand that everything is a play of the same energetic life force or creative principle. Everything is only playing a role for us to keep progressing until we see that oneness. When we start seeing darkness in others or judging others, that is when we get caught in this minefield of creating differences among ourselves. It is important for us to understand that both the good and the bad are equally part of that same Divine Consciousness. The whole idea is to go beyond and above.

It's like a rocket. When it gets ignited, it requires maximum thrust and power in order to leave gravity. As it keeps going up, it starts experiencing less and less inertia and is able to leave the atmosphere of the Earth. The force of gravity pulling us down are judgements, opinions, calling names and taking sides. They manifest when we don't understand that everything is that same one principle, that same one Consciousness. Once we start to go higher and higher up energetically and in our understanding that all the so-called duality is nothing but oneness, we get into an orbit beyond the atmospheric pressure of the planet, where there are simply no pulls and pressures that bind us down. That is the state of equanimity or *Sthitaprajna*.

We will keep moving steadily into that as we change our views regarding people and situations. In this world, everything is beautifully and perfectly designed and brought into our life just to extract the best out of us. On our own, we would never want to face hardships or problems; the so-called problems are brought in for us to progress into the next stage.

CHAPTER 11: AN IMPERFECTLY PERFECT WORLD

We have said that in this universe there are always two opposing forces, one working in our favour and the other working counter to it; and that the whole dance or game of life is played between these two opposing forces. That is how we grow and how we become better versions of ourselves, which is the objective of this life. We have also spoken about the law of the creative life force that everything is energy and how the energies move in two different directions. This is how the energies interact with us and all of creation happens in this interaction. Now, we will be talking about a finer and deeper aspect of that, till we clearly understand who we are, what this world is, what our role is in it and why we are here.

We are going to talk about another very interesting principle, which is that of the 'perfectly imperfect world'. We have always been saying and complaining that this world is not perfect, which is true. It was never meant to be perfect. Yet, at the same time, it is also perfect. How can this contradiction exist? How can there be perfection in imperfection? The Upanishads say:

Om Puurnnam-Adah Puurnnam-Idam
Puurnnaat-Puurnnam Udacyate
Puurnnasya-Puurnnam-Aadaaya
Puurnnam-Eva Avashissyate

It means that this universe is whole and complete by itself. All that is in this universe is a representative of the whole; and so, by its very nature, is whole and complete as well. Each one of us and everything that exists in this universe, all living and non-living beings, are whole and complete. This tells us that it is perfect, but it may not fulfil our definition of perfection because for us, perfection is when everything works perfectly for us. Right now, the world is actually perfect, but in its own imperfect way. It is not imperfect in the eyes of the Creator, but imperfect in our eyes because our expectations are different. However, to the Divine Creator, everything is moving absolutely in perfect order, even the wars, the earthquakes, the floods etcetera.

So, why is life on this planet so chaotic? We know that we have come onto this Earth to grow, evolve and reach a state of perfection in which we experience the Divine Consciousness, we experience the creative life force and we experience the Creator within us. Now, imagine entering a university with the intention of learning and growing, but everything in the university was perfect, including us. Would we be able to ever learn anything? Obviously not! So, the curriculum in a university is designed in such a way that we have to constantly acquire new knowledge and develop skills so that we can put the new knowledge into practice. Whether we have learnt or not, and whether we are able to apply the knowledge or not, it is tested with exams that reflect our progress and finally lead to our graduation from the university.

The heavens (higher realms spoken of in all religions), where one just enjoys everything, are inhabited by divine beings (*devatas*); but even they have to come down to Earth if they want to attain perfection i.e., to experience their true divinity. This is the planet where we work towards experiencing our perfection, our divinity. Each one of us has come here because there was something lacking in our perfection; something was pending in our learning and understanding and so we came here to complete that course. Therefore, I say that if we are completely involved in this *Parayanam* (intense focussed approach towards the goal), in the next 30 days we may be completing the curriculum that started many, many lifetimes ago. So, the whole idea of this life on this planet is to complete our experience and understanding of who we truly are; and that completion cannot happen if everything were to be perfect around us. Perfection does not leave any scope for learning; imperfection does. Hence this world is perfectly imperfect to enable us to learn and perfect ourselves.

The Earth is like a Shaolin school, where you learn through adversity and challenges to grow and become a better person, in order to graduate and complete the journey. Although to our mind, life on this planet may appear to be imperfect, in the eyes of the Creator it is perfectly set up. Perfection is born in the womb of imperfection. In a hostile environment, peace comes in. In a world full of chaos, order is created. This is how life has been set up here and that is why we have to make the effort to move beyond our ignorance, our wrong understanding, to really know what life is all about and how we are connected to this life. Having understood it, we then start to change the way we look at life.

Our challenge has always been only in our mind. It's the mind which has always created all suffering, all misery, all problems and challenges. These exist in our mind because our mind has different expectations from life. When these expectations are not fulfilled, the mind gets upset and angry, restless and anxious; but if we understand that this life is a beautiful play and everything has been created so beautifully, then we maximise our lessons in this university of Earth. If we approach life with a clear understanding of what we are here to achieve and how everything is actually helping us, the whole way in which we look at things certainly starts to change. The world may appear to be imperfect to our eyes, but it isn't. That is why the Upanishads say that the world is perfect, whole and complete, and so is each one of us. It's just that we are not aware of it, that we have not experienced it yet, so we keep coming again and again onto this planet.

What we are seeking in each different lifetime is this perfection, this completion. I hope this will be the last time that we seek it. Our present approach towards it is of a *Parayanam* (committed and dedicated approach) and not a normal, casual *Satsanga* (simple gathering of seekers/knowers of truth). If we are really seeking, if we are really keen, if we totally believe in it, then we must be able to commit ourselves fully to it. Our commitment to this process is critical. There will be challenges and we will also be tested on it. There could be commitments which may come in conflict with this, we could be tempted to attend some other meetings, other things could lure us, some pressures could come to us, or any other such challenge could confront us. The choice would be clearly in our hands; we will have to make the right choice. If we give this the importance that it is demanding and if we think this is what the goal of our life is, then I do not know if there can be anything more important in our lives at this moment than to focus on experiencing our own truth, our divinity. That is the reason why we called it *Parayanam*. This is where we are committing ourselves to be, because we are absolutely and keenly wanting this to happen. Without that wanting, without that single minded desire for liberation, for *Moksha* or enlightenment, it's not going to happen. But if we get completely immersed in our Self, we will start experiencing those aspects of our being which we have not experienced so far.

These times are prophetic. They are magical times where, if we yearn with our heart, mind and soul, there is absolutely no reason that it will not happen. Let us have absolute clarity in our mind that there is nothing wrong with the world, with the times or with what's happening in the world. Everything is perfectly ordained and is perfect in its imperfection for us to become perfect. If everything in our house is in order, then where is the need to do anything? If everything is going well in our offices, where is the need for us to make an effort? The whole idea of making an effort is to overcome that which is appearing to be not so perfect.

If in these initial days, when we are making an effort to remember the truth of ourselves, we remain as an observer of this truth, as an experiencer of this truth, we can rest assured that towards the end of this journey things will become effortless. We will clear all the filters in our mind and our senses that have made us perceive this world differently than how it is. Then, we will be able to start enjoying the perfection of this universe.

CHAPTER 12: SOLUTION WITHIN A PROBLEM

In Chapter 12, we will keep going deeper and deeper till we completely understand that whatever has happened in our lives has been perfectly ordained and has been perfectly designed for our specific needs so that we can grow. As long as we do not understand it, we remain ignorant about it and think of it as a challenge, a problem, or a source of suffering. But as soon as our perception shifts and we understand what is really happening to us in our lives, our awareness shifts, the penny drops, and something new opens up. We start looking at every problem or challenge as a lesson for our growth.

We have been talking about challenges, but now we will be talking about solutions. Every problem, every challenge, every adversity actually has a solution rolled up inside it just as the quietest part of the storm is at the centre of the storm. All the challenges that come to us are sent by none other than our own creative life force; but they come only because the creative life force knows that we can handle them and that we are good enough to face them. All we need is to find the solution, which the creator has already packed within the problem itself.

However, what happens with all of us is that we start focusing so much on the problem that we don't pay attention to the solution. We should learn how to deal with problems. Whenever a challenge comes in our life, first we must accept that there is one, instead of trying to deny it, fight it or put the blame on somebody else. We must accept that it has come because it is time for us to grow. Life is about practising to become a better version of ourselves. We are practitioners of life, not theorists of life. We must live life in practice, not in concept. This means that we have to live life in such a way that we experience the truth of ourselves (*Sat*), we remain in the awareness of who we truly are (*Chit*) and we experience the bliss that we call *Ananda*. We should not live merely knowing the concept of *Sat Chit Ananda* but must experience it as well. And, unless we experience this in its totality, the bliss that we are seeking will not come to us. For this we need practice or *Nididhyasana* which is a very important aspect of our learning and growth.

Our objective is to become skilful practitioners of life. For e.g., if we want to understand what it's like to be a yoga practitioner, we learn yoga, we become good at it, we become a yoga instructor and then we keep practising it to become a better and better yoga instructor. This way, we become more and more skilful at yoga. In life too, we have to become more and more adept and skilful at what life is all about. As we become proficient in what we do, our entire day gets filled with small, small perfections because we start doing everything perfectly. There is a joy that automatically arises when perfection happens. Even simple things like making a perfect cup of tea and drinking it, gives us joy. When we make food perfectly or fold our clothes nicely and perfectly, it gives us a lot of joy. That journey of how to become skilful practitioners, where everything is done beautifully even if it is solving a challenge or a problem, is what we are beginning to get into. Problems are going to come, and we are the lucky ones to whom life keeps throwing challenge after challenge to become skilful so that we can grow.

I recall one particular part of Bhagavad Gita, when Kunti, who was the mother of the Pandavas, actually prayed to Shri Krishna saying, 'Oh Lord, I remember You the utmost when I have challenges and problems'. So, when Krishna asked what boon she wanted, Kunti said, 'Oh Krishna, please always give me challenges and problems, so that I constantly keep remembering

You and never forget You till the last day of my life'. We are not saying that we want problems all the time; we are saying that, when the problem comes, we should have the right attitude in order to tackle it. We have to accept that it has come to us to make us grow and become more skilful.

Let's look for the solution. All life on this planet is energy, and this energetic life force is inside of us and around us. This energy is just one, but if it comes from a person whom we like, we say it is good energy and if it comes from a person who we do not like, we say it is bad energy. Actually, energy does not have a quality; energy is energy. It is the human mind which puts it into the category of good and bad, creating labels around it. If the energy is the same and it is everywhere, then we are equally the creators of this energy because we are that energy as well.

Therefore, we have to start looking at life from the point of view of being creators of this energy rather than victims of it. There is no need to struggle and have the attitude of being a victim of it. Our attitude should be to look at it as an adventure, as a challenge and an opportunity to grow. We must look at it as a way of becoming one with that creative ability and that creative life force which we truly are. The reason I keep stressing it again and again is because, hopefully, it will go into our *Manana* (conscious thinking/awareness) and we will start feeling, and practising that we are that. Once it becomes our awareness, we will start having the experience.

If the experience is not coming to us, it is because we are not marinating in this thought and remaining in this awareness. Once it comes into our awareness, it will automatically become our experience. Contemplation is necessary for this. When we read a book for 30 minutes to one hour in a day, what we do in the next 23 hours to assimilate its knowledge is most important. *Manana* (contemplation) is crucial to see how we can remain in that awareness which requires practice. This practice is not physically doing anything, but reminding ourselves constantly to be aware, to be alert. Once that awareness comes, all experiences start to shift. Blame and judgement dissolve and we start experiencing love. All negativity goes and positivity starts to come in. So, it's important to look at a problem with the right attitude. We should consider it a friend, actually our best friend, who has come to nudge us forward so that we can focus on the solution. Remember, the solution is always there.

This is similar to the story of God saying, 'Man will be sent onto Earth to experience his divinity; but if it is too easy and he can find it everywhere, then he would have no challenge at all'. So, when the *Devas* (divine beings) asked where this divinity should be hidden to make it challenging, God said, 'Let's put it inside the heart of man. He will start looking for it everywhere on the outside, while it is actually inside of him.' In the same way, we are never given a problem that we can't handle or overcome. The key to the solution is always in the centre of the problem. If we look at it as a challenge, we will instantly see the solution. When this becomes a game and an adventure, it brings joy and the next time a new challenge comes our way, we will be confident enough to handle it with the right perspective. This is the whole essential understanding of Bhagavad Gita.

Karmanyeva adhikaraste ma phaleshu kad achana,
Ma karmaphalahetur bhurma te sangostvakarmani.
(Bhagavad Gita Chapter 2, Verse 47)

It means that 'you have the right only to work, but never to its fruits. Let not the fruits of action be your motive, nor let your attachment be to inaction'. In our context, it simply translates as, 'We must do all our work and respond to all situations to the best of our ability. We should constantly strive and make our best effort under the given circumstances; neither for a particular result, nor for expectation of any reward, but do it as our duty, since inaction is not an option'.

Then our attitude towards life changes completely; we no longer complain, we are no longer a victim and we no longer want to run away from the problems. Instead, we skilfully deal with them, and we become skilful practitioners of life and its principles. When a problem arises, if we get into a panic, feel anger, disgust or any other strong emotion, that is when we start to become negative. Once a negative thought or emotion comes, it is so strong that it transmits through our entire body and we start becoming fatigued, stressed, and disease comes into us. But, as soon as we change the problem into a challenge and we bring the excitement of a climber who is going to reach the peak of a mountain, the adrenaline starts pumping and the fatigue and the stress get replaced by an unknown sense of joy. We become good at playing this game, we become adept. We start becoming equal minded and it doesn't matter to us if there is a problem. Remember that the Creator will keep throwing challenges at us till we stop reacting to a problem as being a problem.

As soon as our reaction ends and we see things differently, there is no need for these problems because we have understood the hidden lesson. Situations will occur and reoccur again and again so long as the lesson is not learnt. But once we learn the lesson and we stop reacting, that lesson is certainly no longer required. This is the cycle of learning. We must understand the proper rationale of how this cycle works, why we have to complete it and why we must do it ourselves and not get it sorted by anyone else.

This is how our discrimination grows, our attitude towards life changes and slowly brings a shift into our consciousness. If we don't see a problem as a problem or a challenge as a challenge, and if we don't define something which is out of the ordinary or unexpected as an adversity and we change the way we perceive it in our mind, then we have re-languaged our mind. We no longer react; we seem to be always under control when life throws something at us which impacts not only us, but also the people around us. This is a very important insight and we must understand it fully to enable our perception about life, events, and people around us to become crystal clear.

By thus removing the layers of misconceptions and confusion from our minds, we will be able to see them as the light which they truly are. We will come to a point where we will realise that *isavasyam idam sarvam yat kinca jagatyam jagat* (Isha Upanishad, Mantra 1) - there is nothing other than this energetic life force, this God, this Divine Consciousness, which is present everywhere in each one of us. However, we have to keep clarifying the things that trouble us, which force us to judge, to distinguish between good and evil, which force us to create two sides. We must start to see where the challenge arises, where the perception changes and how we can start solving it. As we said, the root cause of all these judgments are our thoughts, and these arise in our mind, which means we have to start applying the solution in our mind. We have to know how to tackle that which upsets us, how to change it completely, and once we become skilled at this, then life's a breeze. When we can say to life, 'Come on, bring it on, let's see what you have, I am ready!' joy spreads, we smile inwardly, and we say, 'It's okay. This too shall pass'.

This *Parayanam* (period of commitment and dedication) is a Divine *Yagna* (vedic ritual). Our devotion and sacrifice for these 40 days is very important because it will unleash in us a potent and indescribable power that uplifts us and takes us where we need to be. The mind is very tricky, it will keep giving us excuses and, when the negative reasons don't work, it will give us very positive reasons like selfless service and good work to try and keep us away from following the true path. These are all temptations that come in different ways. Remember that *Maya* (illusion) keeps tempting us, but we, as seekers of truth, need to make our own choices which aid our progress.

CHAPTER 13: SELF

A beautiful welcome to everyone on day 13. Today, I am conducting this session from a very holy and most beautiful place called Tiruvannamalai, which is the *Ashram* of Maharishi Ramana. It has been an amazing experience. I have been having this pull of visiting the Maharishi in his *Ashram*. We travelled at 4am and, after just 3 hours of sleep, I am absolutely and fully charged, having had the most divine experience of that one Consciousness and the presence of the Master.

Though I often experience his presence, there was a calling to come here today. The last time I came was in December 2015. So, exactly seven years later, I am again in this holy place and I can only say that what happened today was magical. The call was so strong and the way the program happened was so sudden, that I knew I had to be with him today. I am here sending you all the loving energies from the Ramana *Ashram* and the great Master, and I hope that you will receive his blessings and that his energy will travel to all of you through my words. These are not my words; I am praying to Maharishi to take over and inspire today's session. This session is dedicated to him and his message. As you walk into Maharishi's *Ashram*, there is only one message very boldly written on the walls; and that's the story of how he achieved Self-realisation.

The story goes that one day, when he was 16 years old, he suddenly felt the very uncomfortable feeling that he was about to die. Though he was actually hale, hearty and healthy, he suddenly had this overwhelming feeling that death was near. So, what he did was simply lie down on the floor to experience what death was all about and, to aid it, he pinched his nostrils and tried to hold his breath. His body became stiff and he tried to pretend what it felt like to be in the state of rigor mortis. He imagined what death would be like. He wanted to experience first-hand how it feels when you're dead. In that experience, he found that the body dies but there is something which doesn't die and which still has an awareness. Though he could see his body becoming stiff and not breathing, he was experiencing everything. That made him realise that the real Self was not the body. There was this awareness, there was this Consciousness which was ever present. Therefore, he realised that the body was an illusion and was just holding onto something which is the real Self.

From that day onwards, he discarded all the ideas and notions of the body and started to abide in that awareness. He would absolutely ignore all the thoughts that crossed his mind and not react to them. He would let the thoughts come. He did not fight them, he did not try to control them, he did not try to change them. He simply realised that he was neither the mind nor the thoughts. After having this experience, he refused to be drawn into the world of the thoughts and the body. So, he would just sit and meditate and remain in the awareness of that Consciousness. That's how naturally it came to him, by steadfastly abiding in the Self and ignoring the battle that was going on in the mind. By simply not reacting to the thoughts that were coming in and by just remaining in that state, he became Self-realised. He understood the Self was neither the body, nor the mind, nor the thoughts, nor the feelings and emotions which constantly tug at us.

Whichever thought we feed and give attention to grows and manifests. *Yad bhaavam tad bhavati*; that's how everything starts happening for us. Remember the example I gave you of this screen where Sri Sathya Sai Baba showed me how our thoughts get projected onto it and create *Karma* (the cycle of cause and effect). If we get attached to those thoughts, if we give meaning to them, then the whole cycle of *Karma* starts to operate and we get caught in either enjoying the fruits of our actions or suffering the consequences of them.

Maharishi Ramana understood that the body and the mind were separate from the Self, and that the real Self was an observer. It does not die. Death comes to the body and to the mind, but the Self remains. He instantly freed himself from all the plays of the mind. He remained silent and became liberated. Now, this may sound very difficult but it also appears ridiculously simple. He had the advantage of having the relatively unconditioned and open mind of a young boy of only 16 years, unlike ours which are stuffed with opinions, judgments and experiences and make us really inflexible. He was not interested in the tricks of the monkey mind and just stayed away from it.

It's worth giving it a shot. Because we are now in this *Parayanam* (devotional journey), we are also putting in that effort, we are bringing willpower and the force in us is getting expressed. This force is everything; it's just that we have never tapped into our latent force or energy inside of us. We have not used this *Ichcha Shakti*, the will power through which everything was created, through which we can send light, healing and love.

Maharishi Ramana is inspiring us today with these words and this very simple message. In the silence I experienced the whole day, there was nothing else to be expressed. All that I had to receive I received, all the energetic balancing that had to happen happened; and I was in a state of absolute equanimity. Something was triggered and I have absolutely no words to express it. With the grace of the great master, this seed has been planted. I can only add a prayer that the seed of the truth which is expressed so simply grows quickly, as it falls in fertile ground. It's a prepared ground, because we have been working on ourselves and we are ready to receive it.

I had actually planned to talk about something in

continuation from before, but I honoured the message that was coming to me and I honoured the presence here. I have travelled here on behalf of each one of us because we all are one. I have always honoured what the inner self tells me; I never question it or doubt it. I act on it, because I've realised that when I act on it everything starts happening. You know you'll reach your destination and you know who will come along with you. At every point of time, you start having the experience that the universe is waiting for you.

Since it was Sunday morning and there was much traffic, everything was quite chaotic; but as we reached the *Ashram*, a car came out of the only parking space available and we got the slot. That's how things flow when we are in a state of surrender. Without a plan, everything materialises because we are open and we are not putting our mind to it. People keep thinking and making plans and it's OK to make plans, but I have learnt something else. To live in the moment and, when the present gives us something, we just take it. Yes, we should use the mind to be absolutely clear and execute the plan with perfection, but we must act from the heart. As I have shared earlier, belief turns into faith, faith turns into knowingness and knowingness turns into beingness. Then, we know that Consciousness is waiting for us, waiting to receive us and guide us to where we need to be. So, when we know that the universe is creating it all, the journey becomes very beautiful.

I hope that today you are receiving the vibration and the energy of joy that I am experiencing. It's a joy like none other. May this energy and these words have the impact they are meant to have, as willed by the master. So, with that simple and yet profound message of Maharishi, I want to tell you all that I love you and that life is not as complex as we make it out to be. It is actually very profound, simple, meaningful and joyful. May we receive this love coming from the great master and may it always remain within us.

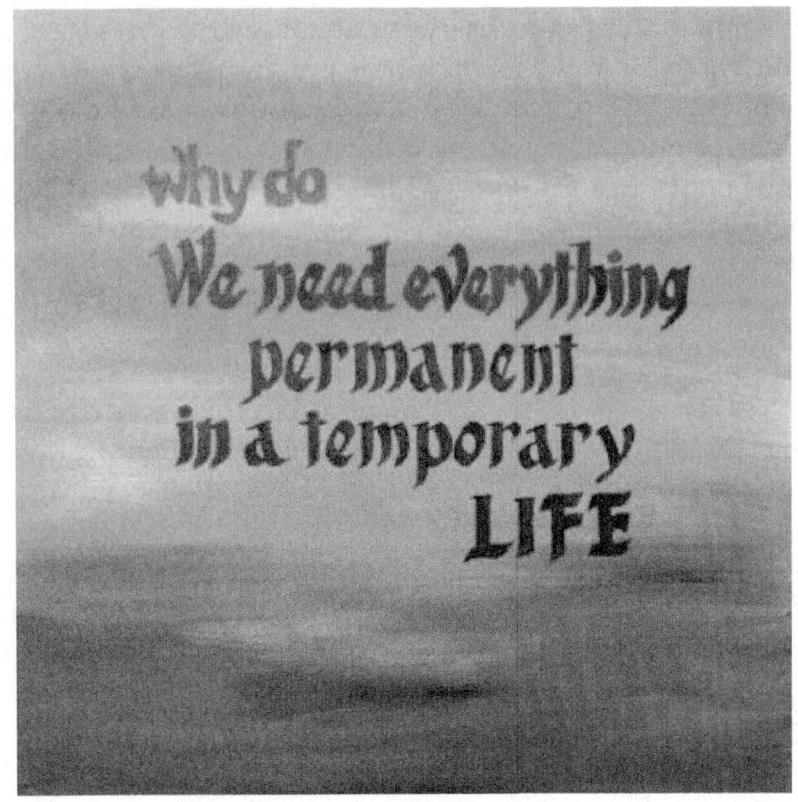

CHAPTER 14: PERMANENCE IN IMPERMANENCE

The Masters and all other forms of Gods and Goddesses appear for those who are seeking and are ready. That is the most essential ingredient: our own readiness, our own preparedness and our own ability to surrender ourselves to these higher forms of Consciousness. Actually, there is no difference between us and them. We are all in a constant state of oneness and union with these Masters and higher beings. They are archetypes of our understanding of higher Consciousness. We give them names and forms which are very pleasing to us and we interact with those forms. Their presence with us is for a reason: to make us experience, in this particular body and mind, that non-dual oneness, which is beyond all differences.

So, now we will be taking our experiential journey forward and picking up from Maharishi Ramana's message that the real Self is beyond the body and the mind. If we remain in the abidance of that Self, if we disconnect and move away from all that binds us to the mind and the body, the *karmic* influences of past actions are rendered ineffective. There is nothing called a mind. The mind is not the brain; it is not physical in nature. How amazing it is that we have been brainwashed over aeons to believe in the mind, when the mind physically does not exist! We are able to believe in our spiritual heart, that does not physically exist either, but we are not able to believe that God is within us.

So, today we are going to talk about the idea of permanence residing in impermanence and bring it into our experience. We have already talked about the contradictions that exist, about oneness residing in duality, about the opposing forces and about perfection residing in imperfection. In the same way, the Self or *Atman* (which is permanent) is different from the *Jiva* (the individual mind and body apparatus) which by nature is impermanent. Like everything else that is created in this world, this apparatus of the body and the mind is also subject to change and so, we call it impermanent.

Nature is constantly changing; the change of seasons being a prominent example. The trees are constantly changing from having leaves, to shedding leaves, to flowering and bearing fruits. There are changes in the human body as we grow from a child's body, to an adult's body, to an old body and, finally, to the state of being no-body. Our physical appearances change. All that we eat to sustain energy in our body also undergoes change. The cells in our body are being created and they are getting destroyed. So, everything around us is constantly changing, everything in our body is also constantly changing, yet the Self remains as it is. As Ramana Maharishi said, it is ever present because it was neither born nor does it die. There is something that is permanent which was, which is, and which remains.

We have all these different Masters and gods and avatars. We have a God for almost every occasion, because we have created them. We gave them energy and they became real. They are as real as we want them to be, and we are as real as they are. Some of us are able to see them, play with them and talk to them. We are ready to believe in them because we see them. But, you know what we see is an illusion, what we hear is an illusion, because it is all coming from outside. They come as harbingers of a message and that message is that 'If you believe in us then you must believe that you are one with us; you are the same as us.' Whenever we experience these Gods, these Masters, that's the only real message for us .

Many people have been asking me about dreams, about seeing these Masters coming into our homes or experiencing their energetic presence. Their presence is only for one reason: to start believing in our oneness with the Divine Consciousness.

We need to completely change our focus from the outside to the inside. Even if we are seeing Sai Baba standing in front of us, we still have to request that Form, 'Please let me see You inside of me. Please let me experience you within me, as me, and not being as separate and other than me'.

As long as these forms keep coming, though it brings us much joy, it still keeps us in hallucination, in separation. We are here to experience oneness; everything else is like children playing and getting excited. The Real does not leave us. It's just that we are so outwardly focused, fascinated and trapped that we are not able to recognise its presence. It does not suddenly appear and announce its presence. It does not come and go from anywhere. It does not come from a portal and does not manifest itself. In fact it is always there, but we suddenly start experiencing it. It is there, it is who we truly are, and we are very close to getting this experience. It can happen any day.

We chose to do this *Parayanam* because we want these 40 days of intensity in order to go within. That intensity will be the last leg, the last effort required to push ourselves into that state of One Consciousness. There cannot be anything more pressing than what we are doing right now for us to come into that oneness, into the awareness that Maharishi Ramana talks about. Once we get the focus and willpower to intensely seek it, it will happen and it will never leave us. Then, no matter what we do, no matter what our body is involved with, no matter what our mind is telling us, we will not participate in it. We will have that clarity and peace. We have been saying that the final experience is *Ananda* (bliss). The experience of Self-realisation is the experience of deep peace and contentment which is uninterrupted, which remains.

When we experience it, we will know what it is, we will be able to recognise it. It will remain with us as we stop getting distracted by the illusory world. Even if we think we are doing God's work or our *guru's* work, that is an illusion, it does not exist. Anything from the outside is a trap that binds us down, for whatever good or not so good reason. However, once we achieve stillness, and the clarity that comes from that stillness, when that which is permanent becomes our experience, we start experiencing a state of uninterrupted and effortless peace and contentment. Then nothing else is required. There is no excitement for anything; and every challenge seems to be as exciting as any joy. That state of oneness where nothing alters us is where we are headed. This permanence is born in this impermanent world only. That is the reason the imperfect world is impermanent; it's subject to change and destruction. So, no matter from which aspect you look at the world, it is illusory in nature. That is why it is called *Maya* (illusion). It looks so real, so attractive, but we must focus on the inner essence of why we are doing what we are doing.

As long as we feel that we must do something for whatever good reason or higher purpose, we are not free, we are still caught up. The minute we become one with our Self, all that we thought was holding us down, was compelling us to cling on, loses its grip on us and we become truly free. That is when the mind no longer creates delusion or compulsion; we become still and the urges of the mind and the discomforts of the body no longer affect us.

Once peace and stillness come, this permanent Consciousness starts to speak to us through intuition and inner promptings, which are very different from our mind. The minute we start sitting in silence and stillness, we immediately start getting prompts from the mind about what we have not done yet and need to do. The mind starts to chatter and become active. At such times, the only thing we need to do is just not pay any attention to it. We do not need to run to a notebook and start taking notes in case we forget something. We just have to learn to ignore what the mind is telling us. When we go into deep silence, when we are in a state of thoughtlessness, that is when our higher Self or the *Atman* speaks to us; that is when the gods and our Masters talk to us. That is the difference between listening to the mind and listening to the Self. Slowly, as the experience grows, we start feeling joy and intuitively follow the promptings from within. We begin to discern between the mind and the higher Self, and the duration of this experience of peace starts to increase.

Consciousness appears when we achieve stillness, when we choose to just ignore the mind. We must understand that the mind is the cause of all our pains, of all our births and that the mind by itself just does not exist. If we focus on the experience of peace every day, then we can experience it all the time. Why does this experience not become permanent? Is it because we are not willing to put in the effort, or we are lazy or maybe there are some other challenges that we are not able to overcome. We need to start getting deeper into what bothers us, into what is still coming in the way of our practising *Manana* (self-inquiry) and *Nididhyasana* (self-practise), because that's the only way to experience peace permanently. We recognise what this experience is, we know what our goal is and we know that we do achieve it a few times in the day or for a couple of days; but now we must find out why it doesn't remain with us permanently. The answer has to come from within and each one of us has to figure out our own connection since each one connects in a different way. Once we get that connection it will never go away.

So, remember, everything is impermanent in this impermanent world. All that is perceived by the five senses is impermanent. The permanent cannot be perceived by any of these senses but what you are going to experience within you is permanent; the permanent within the impermanent.

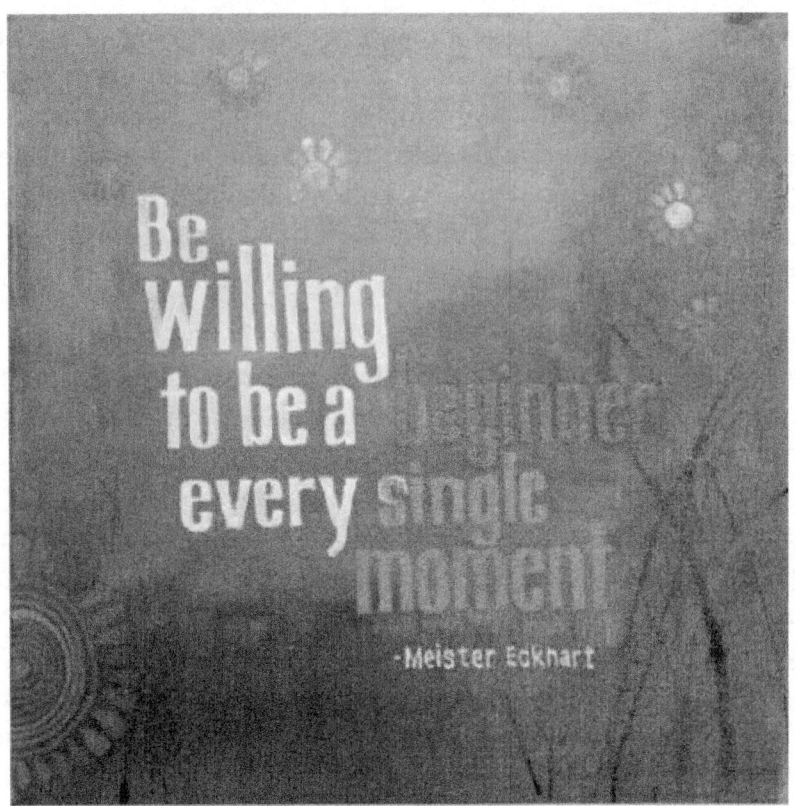

CHAPTER 15: ADAPT GROW AND EVOLVE

In the previous chapter we spoke about permanence and impermanence. The whole world has been created to be a place of impermanence, of constant change. And in that changing world, we take birth in a body to experience that we are changeless, permanent and beyond the mind and the body. We are eternal, we are immortal, we are the ever-present Consciousness. However, we lack first, in our understanding, second, in our experience and third, in our awareness of the same. Understand that what comes and goes is not the Consciousness but the awareness. When the awareness becomes ever present, then we will experience Consciousness constantly.

It is a fallacy to say 'Divine Consciousness' or 'Universal Consciousness', because there is only one Consciousness. We cannot qualify Consciousness by saying God Consciousness, Jesus Consciousness, Rama Consciousness, Sathya Sai Consciousness. That's just our mind trying to hold on to name and form. We are so fascinated with name and form that we even want to put a name to Consciousness and call it something. That is how we have been comprehending things. Our mind always wants an explanation, a name. It always wants to hold on to something. So, for now, let us call it Universal Consciousness, till we know that there are no two types of Consciousness.

Consciousness does not get sullied or soiled if it goes into the body-mind of a person who is a killer nor does it get purified if it goes into the body of a saint. It is always unblemished. It does not have any attributes, it is beyond the definitions of right and wrong, pure and impure, auspicious or inauspicious. It is our mind which keeps categorising it. It is our thoughts which come from our fascinations or repulsions, our sense of romance, our sense of dreams, passions, etcetera. and create an interesting set of emotions. These emotions are nothing but our strong beliefs in something. When a thought acquires a dimension of energy, it becomes a strong feeling. Even the Divine Consciousness is experienced by us as a feeling of an energy even though it does not have any quality associated with it.

So, slowly, as a first step, we start to get into the experience and as it comes we are able to let go of the filter or the strong glasses that we are wearing which colour this Consciousness. We slowly start to see it, as the cataract from our eyes is removed. That cataract is based on judgments, opinions and thoughts stemming from our mind. Currently we are in that process. Every day there is something significant opening inside each one of us; there is a realisation which is coming to us. And that's why these intense 40 days are essential, because they are going to shift things for us. The intensity which is building up is going to carry us through to our destination.

Today, we are extending the discussion even further and we are coming to a very important conclusion, which we've been building up for a while. We will give the final appeal to the mind today, so that it can finally rest in peace, and stop troubling us. Because the mind is used to logic, likes logic and is very rational, we will be giving the mind a logic which it cannot deny, since that logic is based on our experience. We will be talking about the experiences each one of us has had in our lives and the conclusion drawn from these will be logical enough for our minds to surrender.

Let us all look at our lives. We have all physically aged; a number of years have passed since we were born and took a body. Since then, until today, we've had thousands of experiences, dealt with millions of situations and met hundreds of people. We have happy memories, we have sad memories and some experiences we do not remember at all. But definitely each one of us has had a variety of experiences, with a variety of people. If we were to recall these experiences, we will notice that we are able to majorly recall those experiences which had made us feel very uncomfortable and sad. On the contrary, there would be very few memories of happy experiences in our life. Somehow our mind has a habit of holding onto the memories of unpleasant things and happiness seems to get washed away. It's something that the mind revels in, it's very adept at it. That is the reason why we hold on to the negative things in people much more than appreciating all the good things about them.

So, in those unhappy and sad moments, it felt as if the whole world was ganging up against us. During those times, it was very difficult to overcome the experience of grief or sadness, and we would cry, get angry or even call people names. We would feel that life was very unfair and that it was almost impossible to get through that experience. So we used a lot of support from outside. Mostly in India, whenever things don't go well, we go to an astrologer. We seek an explanation for why things were going wrong and once an explanation is given, we say it is because of the stars (in our natal chart) and ask the astrologer to suggest a remedial course of action to appease the unconducive star. We don't realise that it is our *Karma* (deeds) which has led to the bad experience; it is our doing and not the star's. Others may go to a psychologist; some go and cry and take solace with friends or elders. We try to do many different things to cope and overcome those moments of sadness. At such times, the negative thoughts in us are overpowering because we can't see any ray of hope. The intensity of the emotions is so severe, that it makes the experience extremely uncomfortable for us.

Now, if we were to imagine again that period of extreme emotional moments, then either we would not remember some of them or, if we did remember them, the intensity of the emotion would be lost. We arrive at the realisation that we have already dealt with the situation, came out of it and are not experiencing any of it today. Though it felt so real in the past, having experienced such extreme negative emotions, today after 10, 20 or 30 years, we find it even difficult to recall it and even if we do, we say how childish we were then. This tells us that, if it was real, it should have stayed with us even now; but because it was fleeting and it remained with us temporarily for that time period, today we don't even acknowledge it. This implies that whatever is happening to each one of us even right now, all the thoughts and emotions we're going through right now are also unreal, temporary and impermanent. They are just passing clouds. They only become dark clouds when we put emotion into them. We ourselves actually give birth to negativity. When we focus on the problem, on the event and on judging people, it becomes a sad experience in our life.

Every person is just another person, every situation is just another situation, every event is just another event. It is the mind which slots these into a box. We build these matrices, these walls around us, and we start to categorise. We dwell into it, we keep thinking about it and we start feeling unhappy. If this unhappiness was for real, then today all of us should be unhappy because life has given us enough moments to be unhappy about.

However, the very fact that all of us are positively looking at our journey and having our experiences tells us that what we had experienced so strongly in our life in the past is not real. We imagined it, at that moment, to be real. So these are actually just passing clouds. That is why we say, 'This too shall pass'. This phrase came from the wisdom of all those who realised that these are events which are orchestrated by the mind and do not remain since they are not permanent. The permanent experience is the Self.

Every time a situation, an event or interesting people came into our lives, what did we do? The first thing we did was to adapt. We've always adapted to every situation and figured out how to handle it and come out of it. We've successfully negotiated all those unhappy, emotionally strong moments of our life; and therefore, this adaptation, resilience, comes to us naturally. We have grown in our understanding of life and in our understanding of people. We are more stable in our emotions. When we look back, we realise that many times in our lives we have been childish. It means we have grown and evolved. That's why we can laugh at it and call it childish.

To 'AGE' is to Adapt, Grow and Evolve. So, evolution is the natural and inherent process of all living beings. All of us were born in different places, different countries, different economic circumstances; but there is one commonality- we've all had happy and sad experiences. We've had sad experiences that we found almost impossible to surmount; yet, we have dealt with them, we have grown and evolved. The next step that awaits us is the ultimate step; we are just a tiny step away from the highest point of evolution. That last step, which we are yet to experience, is that we are that Consciousness which has created not just this birth, but also this playfield, this whole world in which we are interacting along with our family members, our friends and the rest of the 7.8 billion people.

Let us reflect and do a lot of *Manana* (reflect/contemplate) about how beautifully we are set up by our own Consciousness to be on the verge of experiencing that for which we have taken innumerable births. Reflect upon how clever the Consciousness is and how cleverly it has been giving us experiences, how beautifully we have grown and evolved that we have reached this point where we are at the cusp of living the ultimate experience. Let us celebrate and rejoice because we are all just waiting to cross over. Pennies will start dropping very fast now, since the time is coming. So, welcome to this magical journey of removing all these layers under which we have hidden ourselves. We are removing this cataract from our inner eyes to experience the joy that comes from stillness, from understanding, when the unreal is removed.

We have made beautiful progress in these 15 days. We have reached a major milestone in our understanding of our own journey and Self. We must thank the mind, because it has been a great friend of ours; it has brought us till here and it is now allowing us to surrender to the Consciousness. Today, the mind hands over the reins of our life to the Consciousness. So, a great applause to our mind and thank you for letting go. Gratitude to all the Masters who are channelling their understanding in a very simple and profound way.

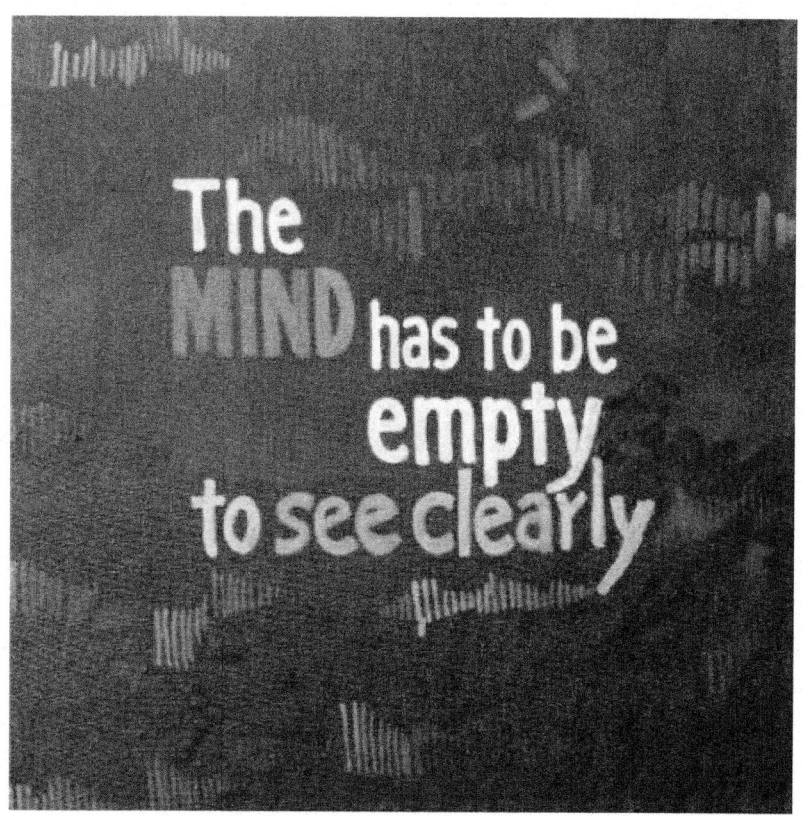

CHAPTER 16: ALL SUFFERING IS IN THE MIND

We have realised that all our past experiences, especially the strongest of them, are not real. They are transitory, impermanent. Anything which is fleeting cannot be real, because it does not fit into the definition of Truth. We are trying to experience the truth of ourselves, which is changeless. Truth means what has been, what is and what shall always be in its unmodified and original form without undergoing any change. Since our bodies and our minds have undergone change, they cannot be real. There is something inside of us which is real, which is the source of all this peace, love and energetic connection that we are now beginning to experience. Consciousness has always been there; it's just that when we are preoccupied and our mind takes hold of us, we become unaware of it. So, Consciousness does not appear or disappear, it is the awareness that appears and disappears.

Now, we will discuss the whole concept of sorrow which we ourselves have experienced, as have all the saints, right from Jesus to Buddha to Shankaracharya. All of them have spoken intensively about it and have concluded that this world is full of sorrow. Shankaracharya ji went one step further and said,

> *punarapi jananam punarapi maranam punarapi*
> *janani jathare sayanam, iha samsare bahudustare*
> *krpaya'pare pahi murare*
> *(Bhaja Govindam - Verse 21)*

We have constantly been experiencing birth and death over many lifetimes. Every time we take a body, we have to go through the darkness and discomfort of our mother's womb.

Each time we come we have to experience sorrow and suffering and only God's grace can help us cross this ocean of sorrow. As discussed in previous chapters, sorrow is something that remains in our subconscious, in our memory; and the happy moments just don't seem to register as much as the unhappy ones. So, do we want this journey to continue endlessly moving from one experience of sorrow to another? As Sri Sathya Sai Baba said, 'Happiness is an interval between two pains', meaning it takes pain for us to appreciate what happiness is.

This takes us to the Law of Duality which says that for light to exist, there must be darkness; for goodness to exist, there must be evil. It is in these contradictory forces that the entire game of life is played. The whole game of creation is based on these two opposing forces.

What is sorrow, what is unhappiness? Is it something real or is it a creation of our mind? Is sorrow real or is the mind that experiences this sorrow real? Mind is surely not real; nobody has seen the mind. We think the mind is somewhere inside our head. Something that we have not seen, we call it the mind. And something that we experience, we call it sorrow. But experiencing is not a faculty of the mind, it is the faculty of the heart. So, how does this sorrow take birth, what is it all about and why do we feel sorrowful? We must examine this so that we can push it out of our mind completely.

When things do not happen as per our expectations and are not very pleasant, we call it sorrow. This implies that there is some expectation; there is something which is not normal that is happening. That means happiness must be our normal condition. To be uncomfortable, we must know what it is to be comfortable. The fact that we remember only uncomfortable moments means that they register in our mind so much because that is not our natural state. That is why it rankles inside of us so much. When something unexpected happens and we dwell on it as a problem, it acquires intensity, emotion, and we start to become unhappy.

We have discussed feelings and emotions. We have talked about how a thought by itself is just a thought; but when we keep focusing on it and putting energy into it, it intensifies and becomes a problem. Since we dwell on this problem that disturbs us, rather than accepting it and looking for a solution, it becomes bigger and bigger and begins to impact us. The starting point of all this is the thought. Even expectation is a thought. So too is an expectation to always be happy. Therefore, all sorrow and suffering are born in the mind. If there is no mind, there cannot be any suffering or sorrow. We have earlier concluded that the mind is not real, but we have allowed it to influence us too much. It alone is the reason why we take a body again and again (are born again and again).

The whole balance of our *karmic* account is actually stored in the mind. The idea of liberation, enlightenment and Self-realisation is to make the mind inoperative. Once we figure out that this mind is an illusion and not real, it suddenly loses its grip on us. That happens when we stop listening to the dictates of the mind and start focusing on the awareness of the Consciousness within us. When this happens, all the *karmic* problems that have been bothering us, all the struggles and judgments that have been troubling us, all the filters of the mind that we have been using to see the world, just go away and we become *Nirmal* (pure). We go back to the state of being childlike, absolutely pure.

When we move into the field of Consciousness, all that has been troubling us suddenly starts to go away and we begin to experience the stillness, the silence, the peace and contentment which is our original nature. We do not deliberately focus on stillness, peace or silence, but it starts to happen by itself when the mind loses its grip on us. We are no longer interested in the noise of the outside world and we start to enjoy the silence so much that we just want to be in that state. We are not trying to make an effort towards it; it is happening effortlessly on its own. We begin to realise that the mind is not who we are and that this whole illusion of life has been created by this duo called the body and the mind.

These two came together when we were born into this world; and as we went to our schools and interacted with our parents and with society, nobody told us about the laws of the universe, about body-mind-intellect-buddhi, about Consciousness and awareness. Thus, we just acquired and inherited everything which had to do with the mind. So, the only way for the Consciousness to make its presence felt was to give us these experiences called 'The Hard Knocks of Life', which we misinterpreted as *Dukha* (sorrow or suffering). It was just a way of waking us up and telling us, 'Hey! There is something else that you are not understanding. There is something that you have completely missed, and I will keep giving you wake-up calls till the time you acknowledge my presence.' That is the way of Consciousness to remind us that this world and this lifetime is not just about the mind even though it is because of the mind that we are actually experiencing this sorrow. So, we have to come and clear this account of the mind and sorrow is just a tool used by the Consciousness to create this whole experience to deliver us from the grip of the mind.

It is for us to understand that actually, sorrow does not exist; we give it wings and add emotions to it. If we understand the source of the emotion, then at that root we can nullify it so that it drops on its own. This happens as soon as we get into the awareness of our Consciousness. Anytime a thought or a strong emotion comes to us, we must bring the light of awareness onto it in that very instant. This light resides in our third eye. It's like the light that the dentists wear on their forehead, or the light that miners use when they go deep below the surface of the Earth. All of us have a light on our third eye, in the centre point between our two eyebrows, and that is the light of awareness.

Wherever we put this light of awareness, the darkness of ignorance disappears. We can mentally switch it on every time something unexpected happens in order to become aware that this problem is fleeting, not real. At that very instant, we will be able to stop it from growing and expanding. When we nip it in the bud it reduces to being just an event which has happened, and we don't need to give meaning to it or brood over it. Instead, we can focus on the solution.

When a problem or a challenge comes, if we accept it, and we begin making efforts to solve it, then in that very instant everything shifts. If we don't dwell on the problem, then it will not grow. It is we who make a problem become larger than life by continuously thinking about it. A thought by itself is powerless, but we give it the power by dwelling on it. The thought gets an energy from within and it becomes a feeling, then an emotion, then a strong emotion, then it sucks us down and saps our energy. But now, we have all the tools, all the understanding and we know exactly what to do when something like this happens.

As long as we are in this body, our *Prarabdha Karma* (deeds from previous lifetimes) is going to play out; but we can stop the operation of the current *Karmas* which bind us. We are now equipped to handle them and become unaffected. The whole idea of bliss is to be unaffected. It is not that problems and challenges will not come; they will come but we will not be affected. We will see them as just another event, one more scene in the play of life. As we are not perturbed or agitated by them, we will become neutral to them. That is the state we have to reach.

Remaining aware during the day is an exercise that we all must undertake. It will help us in our journey. When thoughts come, we will be able to just observe them. There will not be a time when thoughts will not come, but we will not be interested in them, we will no longer run after them. We will not give them the attention that they are seeking and, when we stop giving attention to something, it goes away.

For example, if a child knows that the mother is watching, what does it do? It keeps seeking attention and doing things in order to get the mother's attention. But if she stops giving attention to the child, it thinks, 'Oh, mother is not interested. I won't bother her and will continue playing'. That's exactly the relationship between our mind and our thoughts. If we give them attention, they will keep seeking it in order to keep us trapped; but if we don't pay attention to them, they will just go away. We have to get into the habit of not giving them our attention and bring ourselves into awareness.

Slowly, as this discipline falls into place, we will see the shift within ourselves. As I have explained, this is an experiential journey and everything starts shifting when we start to alter the direction of our thoughts and understand that all sorrow is nothing but a creation of the mind.

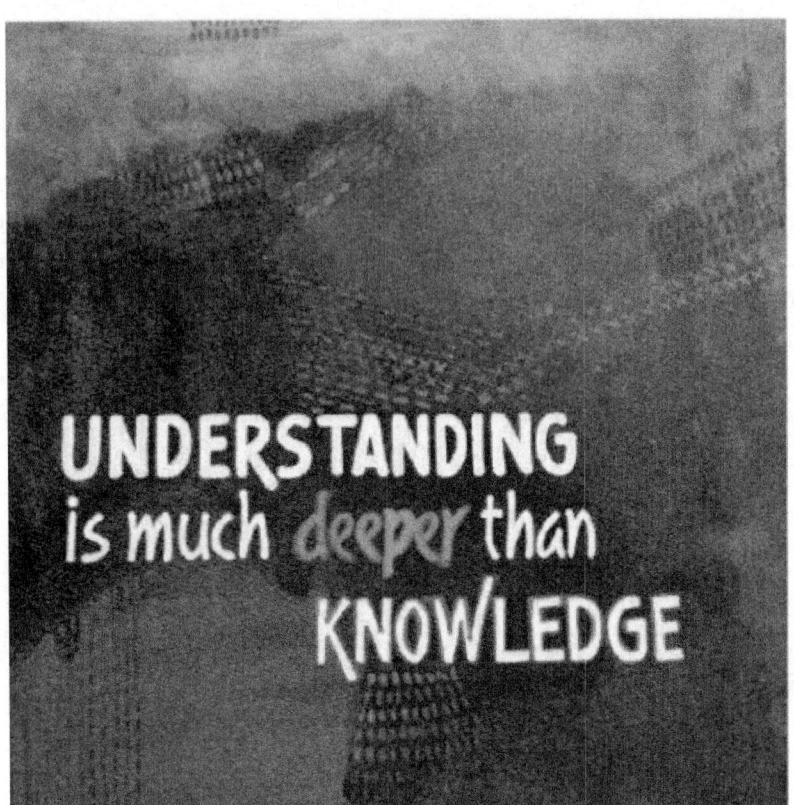

CHAPTER 17: UNLEARN

The mind, which creates all the thoughts and desires, is the reason why we are trapped in a continuous circle of life and death. Mind is rational, intelligent and can differentiate between the various shades; but it does not have the capacity to help us with what we have set out to achieve, which is to experience the Divine Consciousness. We have always said that experience is for the heart and understanding and analysis is for the mind. These two different faculties that God has given us are required; but one of them influences and impacts us negatively, keeping us trapped in this cycle of desires born out of our basic impulses. Mind is the storehouse for all the desires and thoughts and that is why the mind needs to be transcended. When we say that the mind needs to be overcome, we do not mean that we do not need it; what we mean is that for the time being we must silence it, so that we can become aware of our Consciousness. As long as the mind is constantly active, picking up the rights and wrongs, it will never allow us to be aware and experience the Consciousness, which resides inside of us.

It is very much like going to a hospital when we have an illness. We go to the hospital to get well and, during the period that we are admitted there, we stop doing all the things that we normally do in our lives. All the activities we do on a day-to-day basis stop. The food that we eat at home stops, the company of people that we meet stops. Once we are well, we go home and return to our daily routine. This is exactly the case with the mind and the heart. It is because of the mind that we need to go to the hospital to experience our Divine Consciousness. Mind is the daily activities, our usual clutter, our judgments, our experiences, the good and bad that we have been so assiduously storing inside of us. As we are seeking the experience of our Consciousness, we need to transcend and overcome the chatter of the mind, still it and focus it, during this period of the *Parayanam* (intense and dedicated spiritual inquiry).

The mind, which has so beautifully served us till now, is no longer helping us to step ahead. It has become an impediment, a roadblock. So, we need to remove this blockage to go beyond the hump of right and wrong, good and bad. The real Self, the *Atman* or the *Brahman*, is attributeless. There is nothing good and bad, as far as the *Brahman* is concerned. Everything is. There is no duality in *Brahman*. It is the mind which has been categorising everything into these dual experiences. Therefore, to experience that Consciousness which is all pervasive, for some time we need to go away from all that which is impairing the receptivity of that experience of the awareness of who we truly are.

Essentially, we are saying that, to experience what we have not experienced ever before, we need to do something that we have never done before. Using our mind has brought us to a situation where we are stuck in the endless loop of *'Punarupi jananam Punarapi Maranam'* (endless cycle of life and death). We have to get out of this loop and unlearn all the experiences that made us non-receptive to the energetic Consciousness that is within us, around us and in everybody. We need to make the mind subservient to the Consciousness within us.

As our mind is intellectual and analytical, it can only analyse that which it knows; but it does not know what the *Atman* is, as it has never experienced it. Mind cannot be used to go to the end point, and that's the reason why we are stuck in this endless whirlpool. We are using the wrong faculty, and we are not able to move ahead because of this mistake. The *Chitta* is nothing but the memory, a collection of all our experiences, both good and bad. It needs to become absolutely pure, so that we are able to receive all that is happening around us without any filter, without taking sides or putting things into different buckets, which are nothing but prison walls that we keep creating. There are basic feelings and emotions that we have already experienced using the faculty of the mind. However, there is a purer emotion of *Ananda* which we have not yet experienced because we are continuously engaged with the mind.

I would recommend you to listen to *Atma Shatakam* or *Nirvana Shatakam* by Adi Shankracharya. On our YouTube channel, Kailasatheabodeoflove, there are five videos on *Atma Shatakam*, where each of the verses has been taken up in detail. So, for the final experience of *Ananda*, we need to transcend all that which we have become prisoners of. *Atma Shatakam* very beautifully talks about all that which our mind and body have considered to be real, and gives the definition of what the *Brahman, Atman* or Consciousness actually is. It talks about what we are not and takes up every attribute that our mind has put a label on. Somehow, we have believed those labels because of our experiences, which have been reinforced by society.

We have believed that this external world is real and true, but our Vedanta clearly nullifies this and says that everything that we perceive from the mind and the body is nothing but an illusion. This is the illusion we want to get rid of when we pray *'Asato ma sadgamaya'*. The unreal or untrue understanding has come to us because of our collective experiences as individuals, as a family and as a society. The faculty that we have used so far to collect this information that we have classified so beautifully in our *Chitta* (power of perception) is the mind. This mind which has brought us so far is actually the root cause of the continuous cycle of birth and death. Our goal is to finish this cycle.

It is like a game of Ludo, where we start to roll the dice and ultimately come out of our house to complete our journey; or the game of Snakes and Ladders, where we have to go through various steps, getting either rewarded or penalised, until we reach the end. Similarly, in life we need to clear this course; and at this stage we are trying to understand that the mind is not the faculty which will give us the experience of the Self. As soon as the experience starts coming, we will start understanding how the mind has been interfering with it, given the background that we've had.

So, let's consider these 40 days as a period where we are moving away from the mind and trying to get attuned to the faculty which will give us the experience and transform the way we have viewed the world so far. We have to keep ourselves in the awareness that the mind has been interfering in our experience of Consciousness. It is the mind which distracts us from the awareness of the Self, and it is the awareness of the Self which starts to give us an experience we have never had before.

For the sake of this experience, we have to get into the mode of unlearning. Consciousness is always present; it's only our awareness that comes and goes. It's not that we need to learn something more or to acquire any specific skills. We are not talking about a breathing technique or an *Asana* (yogic posture). We are saying that we must shift our focus from the mind to the awareness, in order to experience something that we have never experienced before. Let's not call it anything, let's not put words here, because any debate will be coming from the mind. Since our association with the mind and body is so strong, we must allow space for something which we have not seen but which is there and we can feel. Let's allow ourselves the freedom and the space to experience something new. Let us unlearn and let go of all we have believed in, which may have given us great success in life, in our professions and in whatever we have done so far.

Now, we are getting into a territory where we have never been before. If we keep taking the road to a place where we always go, we will only reach that same place. Now, our goal of life has changed from the accomplishments in the external world to the accomplishments in the internal world. Therefore, this particular faculty that has given us such success in the world is not relevant and will not take us anywhere. In fact, it will keep arguing and giving us reasons for us not to go inside. We will remain poised at the edge of the pond and never jump into the water. Therefore, we will never learn how to swim.

This is a stage of unlearning, of letting go of all that you believe in. All that has put us in good stead has to be kept in lock and key for a while so that we learn another skill, another language, which is the language of the heart, the language of the soul. Once the experience of the language of the heart starts to come to us, we will begin to differentiate between the mind and the soul, and we will understand how the paradigm works inside out, rather than outside in. That is the time when we will go back and open the lock of the mind once again, and bring both the mind and the Consciousness into harmony. We'll synchronise them back again and live life with a new perspective.

There is a beautiful saying of the Upanishads, *'brahmavid brahmaiva bhavati'*, which means that anyone who knows Brahman and remains in the knowledge of Brahman verily becomes Brahman. So, that is the essence of what we have embarked upon. We are all together trying to reach that point where the mind does not interfere with the experience of the Truth that we are seeking. The mind is simply not capable of getting this experience; it is the heart. As long as the mind keeps giving its own twist to things, we will always be on the side-lines and we will never go ahead and jump into the experiential part of the journey and without the experience we will never know it. So, with that appeal to everybody, let's put all our academic knowledge and rationality aside for a while, and go in into this deep, introverted, internal process of experiencing that beautiful energetic presence called Consciousness, that energetic field which has a higher vibration, because all energy ultimately is a vibration.

All those who understand science know that, be it red, violet or green light, it is simply energy at a different level of vibration. So, it's the vibration which gives the colour. Energy is nothing but a vibration, and we need to reach that level of vibration where we become one with this Consciousness. For that, the mind has to be silenced till it hands over the command to the Consciousness. Then, we will start experiencing deep eternal peace, which is the goal of life, which is what we have come here to experience.

CHAPTER 18: BRAHMA SATHYA JAGAT MITHYA

The *vedantic* truth spoken by Sri Adi Shankracharya which we are going to talk about today is *Brahma Sathya Jagat Mithya*. That's the principal exhortation of *vedantic* life and is where our journey starts. Sri Adi Shankracharya says that what we see as *Jagat* (the world) is what we perceive through the mind and the five senses. Our city, world, country, friends, home, garden, pets, the vegetation, all the world which is on fire and fighting, all the world that is so loving, all is an illusion; it is not real. That Brahman or Consciousness which pervades every atom and every living being, which is the cause of creation, which is present both within us and outside of us and vibrates in each one of us at different levels, that alone is real. Consciousness alone is the truth. It is the supreme intelligence. It is who we are and what we shall ever be. It is the source from which we come and we carry it within us. That source is the constant which has always been and shall always remain too. And we have come in this world only to experience this Consciousness.

In this world of impermanence where everything is changing, Consciousness alone is changeless. Once we start getting attuned to this, we begin feeling as if we are at home in our own surroundings. When we are at ease with ourselves and comfortable with our feelings and our emotions anywhere and everywhere, that is when we are truly at home. It is then that we experience the two indicators of *Shanti* (peace) and *Santosh* (contentment), which are interrelated. Only when we start feeling contented and satisfied, do we start experiencing peace. It comes when we do not seek anything, when we have no inner desire to either do something or be somewhere. Yet, once the connection with that home of unbroken peace is established and when an inner prompting commands us to do something or to be somewhere, we just go and do what needs to be done.

Now, this may be confusing and some may ask what is the difference between the urges coming from the mind and the promptings of the inner Self. I will give a small example of how it works so that you can start relating it to your daily life. I always use examples from daily life which may sound small and silly. We keep waiting for big things to happen, but actually life is a collection of these small little things. All the small moments put together make a big beautiful life, and that is what is called remaining in the present moment.

The example that I want to share is this: Recently, I decided to make a trip to Mumbai so I went online to book my air tickets. Since I was traveling at a two-day notice, the flights were quite expensive. I knew I had to travel anyway, so I tried to find and book the best possible flight. Three times it happened that I would go through the booking procedure and give my credit card details, but all would be rejected. I had my classes to take, so I left that for the afternoon. Later on, I had forgotten that I still had to book my ticket, until a message came saying my booking had not been completed. Then, I realised I had lost another five or six hours and the tickets would have become even more expensive. So, I started to book my tickets again and, as before, it wasn't allowing me to book. I knew that there was something being shown to me so I just said, 'Okay, instead of trying to book a return ticket, let me book it one way at a time'. Therefore, I first booked my ticket from Bangalore to Mumbai and got the ticket that I wanted in the morning. When I looked for the return ticket from Mumbai to Bangalore, it was even more expensive than the first one. Suddenly, out of nowhere, there was a new flight that flashed onto my screen, and this was at 1/4th of the cost of what I was about to pay. I ended up paying just half of the fare.

So, if our mind is telling us that we must do something now, but the Consciousness has another plan, it starts communicating with us, it starts giving us hints and it will not stop until we listen to it. When the time was right, I got the ticket. I left my home at four in the morning and went to the airport. I had borrowed a friend's car and I thought I would park it at the airport. This was the first time I was parking a car at Bangalore airport for two days. While driving around in the dark, I found the only empty slot, parked my car and got out. I decided to take a photograph of the number of the parking space, so that I could remember it and find the place on my return late at night on the following day. Guess what the number of the parking space was. B-99, and nine is a divine number. In the whole car park, everything was full except for only one space.

This is how Consciousness has a plan for everything. As we start getting connected with it, it starts taking us where we need to be; and the mind does not get involved at all. It is not that the mind is not required at all, of course it is. It is still required to drive the car, park it, etcetera. The urgings of the mind and the urgings of the heart are two different things. The voice of the Consciousness within is not a physical voice; it is an inner knowingness that comes when we start to train this faculty of listening to it. This creates a world of its own. It guides us to such a beautiful set of experiences, and the way it starts constructing life for us feels far more beautiful than the world of the mind.

The expression *Brahma Sathya Jagat Mithya* simply boils down to this: What the mind creates and perceives is a path of Illusion which leads to a world where the experiences are temporary in nature and keep us trapped in sorrow and happiness. As we progress on this journey into the world of love, we will go into the experience of permanence and the world that this permanence creates for us. That is the ultimate world, the ultimate experience and the permanence that we are seeking.

This permanence is not a physical experience. It is what we are going to be moving into, to fully experience what this Brahman is, as we begin recognising what the inner language is all about.

What is this language of the heart? What is it that the heart perceives when the mind becomes silent and subservient to the heart? The essence of the God(s) that we have prayed to in different forms is Brahman. **The essence of Brahman is energy and the essence of this energy is love.** As the lower love, consciousness as *Jiva* merges with higher Consciousness as *Atma,* it becomes One Consciousness - it becomes Brahman. So, this whole journey is from separation to Oneness, from limited love to all-encompassing love, from selfishness to selflessness, from the mind to the heart.

In order to overcome the illusion that Adi Shankracharya talks about, we need to withdraw and detach. For that, we need *Viveka* (Discrimination) and *Vairagya,* (Detachment). We are now getting into the field of *Atma Vidya*, into experiencing the *Atma*. We are going to talk about it, not in complicated words or *Shlokas*, but through what we experience on a day-to-day basis. How can we start experiencing it? How can we start clarifying, refining, so that what we are experiencing is not from the mind, but is the experience of the Self? Once we start recognising the experience of the mind vis-a-vis the experience of the Self, everything becomes clear, all doubts vanish. We have been misled on this path several times. The mind has tried to catch us unaware and has attempted every trick to keep us in its clutches, but slowly we are beginning to see this and to get out of it.

Even the scientists are saying that there needs to be an observer, and that the world is perceived from the eyes of this observer. The world by itself does not exist, it is an illusion. Our Vedas and Upanishads tell us that God is actually an observer. This Consciousness is nothing but an observer; and there is an observer in each one of us as well. So, we go back to the example of Sri Sathya Sai Baba as an observer, sitting and watching that screen and having a good time. As He said, 'If you want to have a good time, come and sit with Me and you also observe.' In a nutshell, it all comes down to being an observer rather than being in the state of doer-ship.

CHAPTER 19: I AM NOT THE DOER

We spoke about how Brahman is the Truth and the world we perceive with our five senses is unreal. The cause of this delusion stems from the fact that we consider we are the body, which brings in the false understanding that, 'I am the doer'. According to Vedanta, this is the root cause of our taking this apparent world to be real. It appears so because, whatever our five senses perceive, we believe to be real and we start acting on that. We start creating a world where it is our mind which keeps guiding us. All our experiences are perceived in the part of the mind called *Chitta*, which consists of the conscious and the subconscious mind. Since we identify ourselves with the body, we are unaware of the fact that there is an energetic source inside of us and we keep looking at the outer world to get answers.

If the scientific world has already proved that the universe is unreal, why don't we wait for science to prove that there is something within us which is the real us? Science will not do that because it keeps examining the external world but not what is inside of us. The medical world also examines the workings of our body in order to heal it. However, the energetic source or the Consciousness does not come under the scope of the study of any science. The only science which deals with it is the science of spirituality, and the faculty of experience is only given to the spiritual heart, which can perceive and feel things. Our ancient *rishis* (sages and seers) were scientists of the spirit (consciousness).

In order to gain that experience, it is essential that we silence our mind and distance ourselves from its urges. This experience is necessary for us to be convinced about the Truth of ourselves. It requires a leap of faith. How do we experience something that we've never experienced before, since we've always been guided by the mind? It becomes very difficult for us to let go of the mind; and we keep rationalising and trying to figure out whether we can reach our goal through the mind, but we just cannot. Therefore, we need to believe either in the Scriptures or in a Teacher. We need to take a leap of faith and decide we are ready to do something different.

The body is not permanent, so it cannot be the Truth because, as we have said, Truth is changeless and remains. So, if there is truth inside us and if it is permanent, then we must experience it. Vedanta says that the root cause of delusion is considering that we are the body. The body was born into a family. Our parents raised it very lovingly and affectionately and gave us a name and a sense of identity. In fact, the day we are given a name and a family name we are actually given an ego. The ego is born when there is a sense of belonging, a sense of identity, and that identity becomes such a big challenge for us because it remains with us. So, our name and everything that we do in our life becomes our CV, our profile, which becomes how the world starts to know us. When we introduce ourselves, we do it with our name, qualifications and accomplishments. That's what we normally do.

To be able to overcome the mind, we must get away from the notion that we are this body. The body is carrying within it something which is changeless and, if we dissociate ourselves from the body, we will see that the Truth of who we really are is concealed within it. If we can hold on to that thought, we will start to feel and experience something which is beyond the mind, something which is the controller. Even though this experience may come for a brief period, it actually encourages us to go further. The whole path opens up in front of us when we taste the presence of a Consciousness which is all knowing, which keeps guiding us and makes us do things which we thought we had no understanding of.

As I have told you many times, I did not read the Vedas nor the Bhagavad-Gita; however, I started to experience things within myself. I started to access a deep reservoir of knowledge and wisdom which comes from some source that seems to know everything. All my knowledge and all my ability to express things comes not from the mind, not from reading but from a source which seems to know everything and can be connected at all points of time. Wherever I am in the world, I am able to access that. In every situation, I am always guided by that ever-present Force. As we know, the three attributes of the higher Consciousness or Divinity are omnipresence, omniscience, and omnipotence. That which is always present knows everything and is able to do everything. Once we start experiencing these three, we know there is a Presence.

In the initial days, we attribute this presence to a *Guru* or a Master. We say, 'Oh, Baba is present. It is due to Baba's grace that this happens'. We first think of it as a Divine Force which is still external to us. Then, slowly, the experience comes that, since this Divine Force is always present, it must be within us. The penny drops when we realise it is us. Even when this body is sleeping or is unwell in the hospital, there is that something in us which is absolutely active.

Going back to the example of Maharishi Ramana, when he had that death experience and his body became stiff and he was not breathing, even then he knew and experienced that awareness which was absolutely alive. That is when the delusion of the body went away. So, to experience the Truth, we need to realise that we are not the body or the mind. There is something which is controlling this mind, which is intelligent and is always present both in the waking state and in the dream state. It is that awareness which witnesses the waking state and is also the experiencer in the dream state. That which observes (the observer) is who we truly are. The body is just a shell in which this real Self is a constant.

So, that's the starting point of removing the false understanding that we are just the body and the mind. We are the experiencer which is aware of the presence of an energetic life force that is not just the breath but actually the controller of the breath, the Consciousness. This is the fundamental starting point of Vedanta which states that the only Truth is Brahman, the ever-present Consciousness, and that the world is nothing but an appearance, the appearance of the Observer. At least now, that has been clarified even by science.

We've reached almost the midpoint of our *Parayanam* and, from here onwards, we will move into an intensely experiential journey because all the foundations have been laid. We've come to a point where we are diving deep into the Self, and we will start doing more inner work. We will be embarking on direct evidence-based work. As I told you, Consciousness is going to test us all to make sure that we have the willpower to carry through what we have set ourselves to achieve.

Useful Tips

Refer to your journals, contemplate and evaluate where you have reached in your journey. This reflection is necessary since we will be moving into the experiential part of the journey now and a strong foundation is a must for it. Assess your progress and fill up the gaps in your understanding, if any.

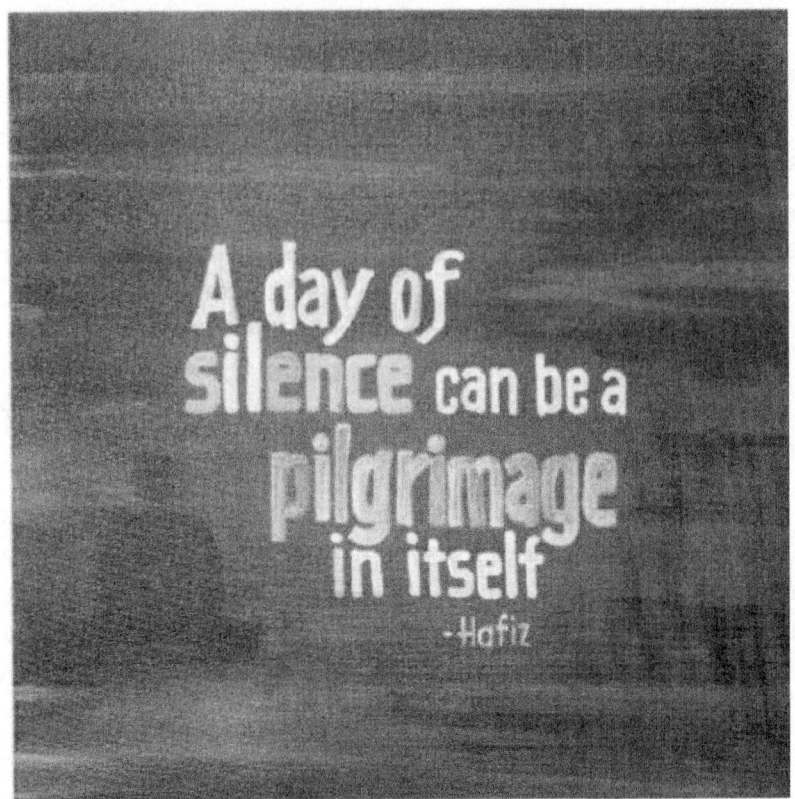

CHAPTER 20: AWARENESS IS THE KEY

Today, we've reached the midpoint of our 40-day *Parayanam*. I thank the Divine Consciousness. I thank my *Guru*, Sri Sathya Sai Baba, for making this happen. I thank all the Masters for guiding us in the infinite wisdom of the Self and I thank everyone for being the reason for such a festival being celebrated.

So, yesterday we spoke about the whole idea that 'I am not the doer'. The illusion of doership comes from the mistaken understanding of being the body. We also spoke about the Self, the Consciousness within.

In the mind we are rigid, but in the Consciousness we are flexible because there is only free flow. We are not bound by any idea or thought. The Consciousness just knows how to communicate. We always remain open. We look at the solutions and the possibilities and, if we are open and positive, everything happens. It adds to the beauty of this journey. When we know everything and when everything is predictable, the journey can become very boring. It is very beautiful how Consciousness starts to relate itself if we are aware of that presence, if we have no particular mind of our own, if we are not stuck to any particular way of being and if we completely surrender ourselves and are open to the possibilities that the Consciousness brings. With Consciousness, there is joy in the unpredictability of life. It's an adventure because we don't know what the next moment is going to bring.

In this journey that we have all embarked upon of experiencing the Self, there is never a dull moment. It's not for the faint-hearted, it's not for those who are stuck up in their beliefs and ideas, which come from the mind. Consciousness has a mind of its own. It is supremely intelligent. It just knows exactly what to do, when to do it and how to do it. Therefore, to experience that, we need to silence the mind. It's not that we are going to let the mind go, we are not going to make such a beautiful instrument useless.

The Consciousness and the mind are in an intimate dance; they dance together like in a tango. Till now, the mind has been making the moves and the Consciousness has been following it; but, to really enjoy what we've come here to experience, the Consciousness must lead the dance. Then, we will enjoy that experience immensely. For some time, we will need to keep the mind aside in order to experience the stillness.

What we will be discussing today is that awareness is the key to transformation. All transformation begins to happen when we start becoming aware of something which we weren't aware of earlier. We become aware that the mind is feeding us with thoughts when we shine the light of awareness on it. Since it is very smart, it does not like to be watched. Like the rabbit which freezes when the headlights fall on it, the mind too freezes when the light of awareness is put on it. It then starts to retreat. When we bring our awareness to the Consciousness or to the heart, and when we stop giving attention to the urges and cravings of the mind, something starts to happen. There is a presence that we start to experience.

The message communicated by masters of Advaita Vedanta like Maharishi Ramana is that everything is preordained and all that must happen will happen, which is what we call the law of *Karma*. Whatever comes to us is actually coming from our past actions. We've already talked about cause, action and effect. So, when everything that comes to us is happening by its own intelligence, where is the question of time? All is happening as it must happen. I had never imagined that we would ever do a 40-day session like this *Parayanam* till we just opened ourselves to it and it started to happen. Today, we are 20 days into it. So, everything is unfolding as it must and that's the reason why time itself becomes an illusion.

Therefore, the best thing is not to react, be silent and observe everything. That is exactly the message Sri Sathya Sai Baba gives with the example of watching the play of the world happening on the screen, when all these thoughts start getting projected. When we start to sit there as a witness and an observer, we become still and, in that stillness, we experience a presence. That presence is the 'I am', the Self, the Consciousness or the Atman. It is always there, it never goes; the only thing that comes and goes is awareness. That means that the key of our transformation is in awareness.

Till a few days back, we were not aware and we thought that the supreme thing was the mind. When we started to go deeper into those moments of stillness, we started to come in connection with that Consciousness, that higher Self, through the awareness. If awareness is there, we remain in the experience and we understand that everything flows from that awareness. Whenever the mind comes in and we start getting involved with thoughts, ideas, opinions and judgments, our awareness automatically goes away.

Therefore, the only way to bring the mind back into the Consciousness is to be aware of the mind and its tricks. The minute we see that we are getting caught in it, we are already beginning to pull it back. So, there is actually no need for any special effort, any special breathing technique or any special *Mantra* (chant) other than being in the awareness of the Self. As we start getting connected, becoming still and observing all that is going on within and outside of us, we stop reacting and getting involved; we withdraw and choose to be the observer, who sits and watches the thoughts coming on the white screen. That is why the Masters have said that the highest teaching is the teaching of silence. All the knowledge, all the wisdom, flows in the silence.

I remember those two years that I would go and sit in the presence of my Master, Sri Sathya Sai Baba. For a week, I would sit in His presence and He would never talk to me. Whatever happened between Him and me took place in silence. Before I could perceive everything in silence, I had to go through a lot of *Shravana, Manana* and *Nididhyasana* (as discussed in chapter 5).

In these 20 days of journey, we are all becoming still. Our experience is in our hands; each one is getting something different, because each one is putting in a different effort. Each one is at a different stage; each one is giving it a different perspective. Words are actually not required, for everything in the world exists in silence, and in silence we transcend the entire idea of time and space. What opens up for us is a brand-new dimension called the dimension of nothingness (*Shunya*); and that nothingness is our real home. In this deep silence, there is no good or bad. There is nothing to achieve, there is no trying. It is just a state of pure beingness where we transcend our body, our mind, our affairs, our relationships and even the entire universe. It is the state of being absolutely free, because there is nothing that is screaming in our head and telling us what to do. We don't have to be anywhere we don't want to be; we don't have to do what we don't want to do. We are in a state of nothingness.

This is the freedom, the *moksha*, the liberation where we are not being forced into anything that we are not comfortable with. This is the feeling of complete comfort, of complete presence, of being at home, that happens when we have reached that stillness, that silence and that nothingness. In this state, there is neither birth nor death, because all concepts coming from the mind melt and we experience this attributeless Consciousness. Only the Self exists and we are that.

We just need to put in the trashcan what we have been carrying so far in our mind, and then permanently delete (do away with) the trashcan because it is only extra baggage on this journey. That is why Baba used to say, 'Less baggage, more comfort'. If we can abide in this nothingness, then we truly experience oneness and, in this oneness, everything starts to happen. A world of its own opens up and true living really starts. A lot of people have the mistaken notion that, when we get connected with this nothingness or this Consciousness, we may become useless to the world and to ourselves; but the truth is that our work truly begins once we become one with that Consciousness. Then, there is no separation left between ourselves, our work, our private life, and our spiritual life. Everything becomes one.

When we express ourselves in this authenticity, how can there be tiredness? How can there be anything that will make us either do something or not do something? We understand how the Masters can keep on helping everyone with an inexhaustible energy. For them, there is no separation, there is no gap between what they think, what they say, and what they do. They have fully purified their thoughts, their words and their actions.

When we just practice and remain in the awareness of this understanding, that is when the experience starts coming to us. Therefore, be still and know that you are God. In our awareness of our Divinity, there should be no other thought and, if we are able to hold on to this thought that 'I am Divine, I am that, I am the Self', then the mind will start to take a back seat. Let us hold on to this truth and surround ourselves with reminders of that, so that everything we touch, everything we see, everything we do, flashes the message that we are Divine.

If in the next 20 days we manage to do this, we will experience a completely new version of ourselves. That's why journaling is so important. Noting down the insights and personal experiences will help us realise how far we have come in our journey. We will be amazed at our progress and will be inspired to complete the entire journey.

All we have done so far is to tell ourselves we are not the body or the mind but the Self, the Consciousness, which is supreme. If we hold on to that Consciousness and remain in awareness, as a witness, we will start becoming silent. We will stop reacting, we will be more in control of ourselves. What we need to know will come to us and we will start to experience the power of the Self. So, that's pretty much what I wanted to share today as a roundup of this milestone that we have reached today. When we go to *Vaishno Devi* in India, we call it the *Ardhkuwari*, which is the halfway stage of that journey. Today, we have reached that beautiful milestone.

CHAPTER 21: ACCEPTING DEATH

There is certainly something shifting for each one of us of which we are going to become aware. All that we need to experience will come to our awareness and we will start to experience something which has always been there, yet we have not been able to perceive it. Our sense of perception is getting far more aware and it really starts to show itself once we become still and silent.

We have realised that awareness is the key to transformation. For anything to start changing in us, we need to bring our awareness to it. However, all this while, whether consciously, unconsciously or by sheer habit, our awareness has been always focusing on the mind, its thoughts and its desires. Therefore, that is the world which we have manifested for ourselves and have been experiencing.

Now, we start to understand that the mind by itself does not exist, as it is nothing but a bundle of thoughts and desires. Yet, it is the mind that has been controlling and manipulating us, keeping us trapped in this play of life. This play is not endless, for a game has a start and a finish. Therefore, this game of life must also have an end. It is this 'end' we are trying to gain an insight about, namely, how to end the game so that we do not have to continue in this cycle of birth and death. The perennial cycle of life and death comes from the mind. It is the mind which creates constant thought, action-reaction, *Prarabdha Karmas* (effect of actions of past lifetimes) and all that for which we have to come again and again.

What we now want to clearly understand is that there is something else which is waiting to be experienced and, once that experience comes, the mind itself just falls away and its manipulations stop and the game ends for us. This is what is called liberation, freedom, enlightenment or Self-realisation.

So, let us now discuss another very important aspect. We have touched on it from time to time, but today we will discuss it at length. It is the concept of death. The holy Scripture of the Sikhs, the Sri Guru Granth Sahib, talks about *'pehle maran Kabool kar, jeevan ki chhad aas'* which means 'First accept death, and let go of the desire to live; then only truly living begins.

Now, what does this mean? There is an undeniable truth – that at some point the body must die. All that was born must die, all that has a form must perish one day. The beauty of life is that we do not know when that moment of leaving the body will come. It can happen any moment. So, if we know that it is a certainty that we are going to die, why don't we just deal with it? Why don't we just accept it?

Death is the most levelling concept. It brings us back to nothingness or *Shunya.* It brings back the whole idea that the body is subject to death, disease and decay. So, if this body is to drop off any minute without any warning, why are we engrossed in life? Where are we caught up? Nothing that we acquire either physically or in terms of our emotions that keep us trapped in happiness and sorrow, is going to remain with us. But most certainly, our thoughts and our desires remain very strongly in our minds and that becomes a reason for our bondage and re-birth.

So, what are we struggling in this life about if we know that this body is going to fall away and is not going to remain? Clearly, the body is not the truth, because truth by definition is what was, what is and what remains. It was in the past, it is in the present and it shall continue in the future as well. Therefore, if the body does not satisfy the definition of truth, it is illusory. If the body is not the truth, then there must be something which is the truth. If the body is a vehicle for this truth to journey in, how do we experience this truth?

Every day we pray that we should be led from the unreal to the real or from the untruth to the truth, by removing the darkness of ignorance. What is this ignorance? It is the ignorance that, 'I am the body and, therefore, I am the doer'. Once this ignorance gets removed, the light of knowledge comes to us and we realise that there is something other than the body, housed within it, which is energetically indestructible, for energy is neither created nor destroyed. Energy always is, always was and always shall be. It is this energetic presence that we are focusing on when we bring our awareness to the higher Self. Everytime our mind starts to think we are able to observe that the thoughts are coming in our mind and as soon as the observation starts, the light of awareness falls on those thoughts, the mind starts to become still. This requires practice (*Nididhyasana*) and attention. When we are aware and alert, slowly and gently, the direction of our life starts to move from the outward to the inward.

Whatever we gain in this outward life -thoughts, opinions, judgements, experiences, wealth, attachment to things and to people-, all of this remains here when we die. We cannot carry our wealth or our loved ones. Thus, death is a very sobering thought. The death of the body, which is slowly creeping towards all of us, can come uninvited at any moment. This fact should help us understand the inevitability of the destruction of this body, and also help us to become clear about our priorities in life. We must ask ourselves, 'Where are my time and efforts going? Are they going towards maintaining attachments to people, things and acquisitions which hinder us to experience the presence within?'

This kind of *Manana* (contemplation) is essential because it serves us as a wake-up call and makes us realise how we spend our entire day chasing that which is temporary, ephemeral and transitory. How funny it is that, out of sheer habit, that is where our attention goes all the time. As we know, whatever gets our attention starts to manifest and grow in our life. Therefore, we are trying to change our way of life from being a way of life on the outside to a way of life which is abiding in the Self, which resides within. As our vision changes from the outside to the inside, we start experiencing that for which we keep coming again and again.

These forty days are helping us to make that concentrated, focused effort in order to experience that which takes lifetimes. The desire for it has been lit in our hearts. There is something in us which is making us look forward to this, which is yearning for that experience. Once that yearning comes in, we quickly start to work towards our goal. Remember that whatever we have worked towards in life, we have been able to achieve. So, there is no reason that this experience is not going to come to us. However, the closer we get to the experience, the more the mind starts to trouble because it sees that it is losing its grip on us and tries to distract and divert us. However, if we are clear about our goal and if we are clear that we are going to make the most of being in the body to the effect of clearing this game of life and finishing it, we will experience that we are the energy which remains always. We will be able to achieve immortality, which is not to the body. Immortality is the nature of energy, for energy neither gets created nor gets destroyed; it always is.

Therefore, once we are clear about what we are seeking, and if in our awareness we are looking for it all the time, then there is nothing in this world that can stop us from experiencing our truth. All manifestations, synchronicities and coincidences start to happen, for there is only one Consciousness; and this Consciousness instantly interacts because there is no other and we begin to get those glimpses of our experiences. So, it all really depends on how strong our yearning is to seek this experience. As we get more and more invested in the idea that the body is not real, that it is an illusion, we will utilise the time that is available for us to investigate the truth of the Self. As we focus our awareness in this higher Consciousness, it starts to reveal itself to us and comes in various experiences.

Coming back again and again to keep going through the experience of getting attached and suffering cannot be what life is all about. There has to be something more to it. We must reflect about that, contemplate about that, and convince ourselves that we are beyond the mind, and if we choose, then the mind cannot have any effect on us because it does not exist. We have given a lot of importance to the cravings, urgings and impulses of the mind till now, but once that stops, the mind stops having an effect on us. Then we start experiencing peace, which indicates the absence of the mind.

Going back to the subject of death, it is the primal source of all fear, and the idea of dying has troubled many people. In many traditions like the Buddhist tradition, they actually talk about death and the art of dying. Death is nothing but leaving one garment and getting into another one at birth. So, we must understand death for what it is. 'Is death to be celebrated or mourned? Is birth a death or is death a birth?' are some perplexing questions to ponder on. If we are the energetic presence, the energetic Consciousness which is universal in nature, then, when we are born, we are actually separated from that energetic source, and we become isolated in a body, and we call it 'birth.' But actually, birth is a separation from our true nature, whereas death, which people fear and mourn about, is actually merging back to who we truly are.

When we reflect upon these things and are able to observe them, it releases us from all the attachments, fears and insecurities that grip us. The sooner we are able to resolve this equation about death and see it for what it is without giving it so much importance, the better. Everyone before us has come and gone; we too shall go and also everyone after us. We do not remember the names of three generations of our elders, and three generations later on no one will remember us. We are so insignificant that even our loved ones to whom we are so attached will not remember us. Yet we are caught up. And because we are caught up, we remain invested in this game.

That is why Shankracharaya Ji said,
'satsangatve nissangatvam (satsanga gives rise to non-attachment)
nissangatve nirmohatvam (non-attachment leads to freedom from delusion)
nirmohatve nischalatattvam (freedom from delusion leads to steadfastness)
nischalatattve jeevanmuktih' (steadfastness gives rise to liberation)

If we remain in the company of truth, *Satsanga,* and constantly keep reminding ourselves of this truth, it brings detachment in us. This detachment slowly removes the delusion about what is real and what is unreal. The removal of delusion helps us to become equanimous. Then, we are not affected by the joys and sorrows of the world. We see everything as it is. We focus on solving the challenges that come to us and, by becoming equanimous, we get liberated. We go beyond the idea of birth and death.

We are looking at the same truth from every angle so that no doubt remains in us and we never leave this idea, get troubled or distracted. The third eye helps us to focus. Our focus on the third eye is to experience the energetic presence. If in these forty days we are able to bring in that focus, then surely and truly the laws that have been holding us back in this world will become no longer operative on us, because we would have transcended the mind. Each one of us will experience that peace and tranquillity which comes from being equanimous. We will see life as a game and remain detached. We will not get caught up in anything, because all our severe reactions come only when we are attached. We will become silent.

When we realise the truth of ourselves, we realise the truth of everybody else because it is the same truth of 'one Consciousness'. So, when we experience *'Aham Brahamasi'* (I am Brahman) then only we can look at *'Sarvam Brahma'* that everything else also in this world is nothing but the *Brahman* (Consciousness).

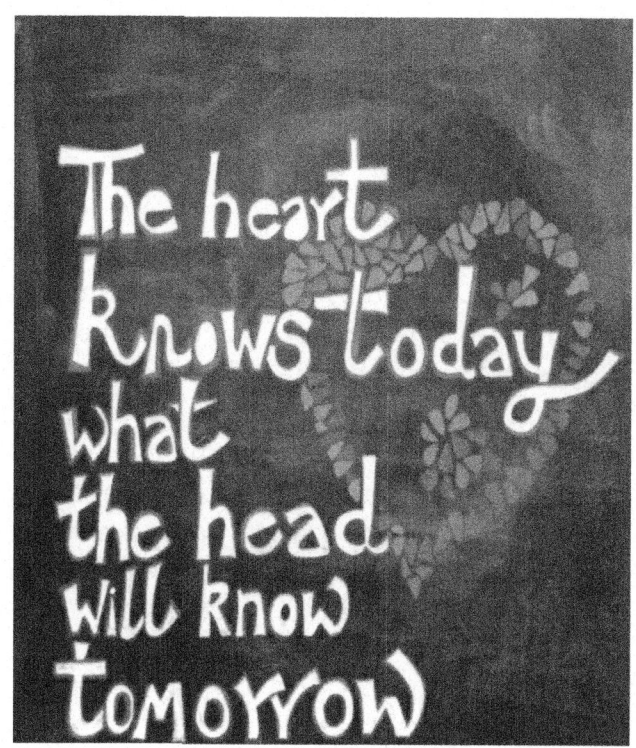

CHAPTER 22: PRESENT MOMENT IS TRUTH

In the last Chapter, we spoke about accepting death, looking it in the eye, and resolving all fears and insecurities around it because death is certain. The only uncertainty is its timing. So, once we realise death is inevitable, we can really start to live our lives. In fact, we need to transform death into a celebration because it is the moment of going home, it is merging back with our source. Why should it be a reason to mourn? It is a myth born out of ignorance, born out of a wrong understanding of life, born out of our understanding that we are the body.

Our ancient *rishis* (sages) understood and experienced that the body is just a bubble and the real Self is immortal. They passed on this wisdom down the ages for all those who are seeking to find out that there is something more to life than being born, growing old and then letting this body go. Is that all there is to life or is there something more to it? So, when we are able to accept, confront and deal with this uncertain and unknown fear that we have of death, we feel liberated; it lightens us up. Just as the body gets purified when we burn/cremate it at death, our mind also gets purified when we examine and accept death and move beyond it. When we root ourselves in the truth that 'I am not this body', there is a light that emanates from us, an unknown force or power comes out of us, which is so strong that its presence can be felt by everybody around us. That is the force of the words that you are receiving now, because they come from that source which is beyond disease, birth, and death. More than the words, it is the energy which transforms. It is the energy through which we perceive and understand.

Our saints and sages sat in silence, knowing no formal languages, and in that silence they could perceive everything. Know that no books are required, there is no need to be wise, no need to have any analytical or oratory skills for this. The Consciousness which is pervading this Universe and which is within us has all the wisdom of the world, and all we need to do is to get tuned to it. To do so, our mind must be silent, clean and clear.

Today, we are going to talk about the inner space that accepting death releases for us. We are all aware that death can come anytime. So, what are we waiting for? The only truth that we know is this present moment. All of Consciousness exists in the present moment. The mind may want to categorise things into past, present and future, but Consciousness does not know any of these concepts. It only knows the present moment. All that is happening is happening in this present moment. Whatever we call the future comes to us only as the present moment. So, the entire world or *Jagat* that we have created as an illusion exists only in this present moment, and will exist in the future only if we are present and are able to perceive it. Once our sense of perception goes, for us, the *Jagat* is no longer there. What a beautiful gift accepting death has brought to us - Appreciation of this present moment because this is all that we have!

The biggest gift that has been given to us is to be aware and present in this moment. So, what we do in this present moment is most important. What are we devoting this present moment to? Are we fully present right now to experience that which we have come to experience, or are we already thinking that within 30 minutes we have to be somewhere else? What is our focus?

In previous Chapters, we spoke about awareness. Awareness is nothing but focus. Where are we putting our attention in the present moment? Are we fully present in the moment or is our mind hijacking us and taking us into something else? Presence is not of the body but of awareness; presence is not of the mind but of the heart. That is the presence being discussed right now. Therefore, the present moment comes to all of us as a great present, as a great gift from the Creator of this Universe. Call Him or Her God or Goddess, call Him or Her by whatever name, because it is neither a Him nor a Her. It is that great Presence in the present moment.

If we can experience today the depth of this present moment, we will understand/be aware that the whole of eternity is in this present moment. It is not important how many years we live. What is important is the awareness with which we live. Most of our lives, we have been living absent-mindedly or in pursuit of this world of attachments, attractions and expectations; but if we were to live just a few years aware of the Consciousness, that would give us the experience that we have come here to seek.

The present moment, this one moment, is very powerful. If we can bring our awareness in this present moment, then liberation or freedom can come in one instant. This is the power of focus that the wise have used in meditation or *Samadhi* (state of intense concentration), or *Tai Chi,* or any of those traditions that various cultures have used for transforming the power of awareness into something greater.

Know that the present moment is so powerful that our entire life and all the thousands and thousands of lives we've had all are present in this one present moment, and we can experience all these past lifetimes in it. Most importantly, if we can remain fully present and joyous in this present moment, no matter what has happened in the past, all the past can be liberated in this single moment. That is the power of the present moment; that is the power of Consciousness. Consciousness itself is attributeless and does not have any negativity. It does not carry any worries, fears or insecurities because all these are created by the mind out of ignorance.

Today, let's tell ourselves that we are going to start practising to live in the present moment, not as a daily chore or activity but as a celebration for a gift that has come from the Creator. It depends upon us how we are going to live it. We can keep thinking, worrying and creating all sorts of possible scenarios to remain completely bound and mired in this world; or we can keep joyously expressing gratitude and sharing our love with all. It will either bring misery or abundance in our lives. The choice is absolutely ours; but the power of making this choice lies in the present moment, for this moment is all there is, and shall ever exist.

When the time comes to say goodbye to this body, we should be so present and so much in celebration that it also becomes a ceremony worth celebrating for all those who are around us. We would have lived such beautiful moments of intense presence that we will not only be absolutely free, but all those who are around us will also get liberated. The key to liberation is in our hands. It does not take chanting of any *Mantra* nor any ritual or practice; all it takes is being ready in this present moment and the belief that all that needs to be done is known to us.

As we open our hearts and come together in this circle of love and light, we start experiencing the synchronicities which make us believe that perhaps there is one Consciousness, that perhaps there has never been any difference between us and that the only thing which has kept us separated is our mind and our opinions. So, I would pray that you free your mind, let go of all that is making you still judge and all the opinions that you have kept locked in your head, and just become like a child which smiles every time it sees something it wants to play with. Let's be like that, as the child does not know any judgement or opinion. It just flows with all that is coming. It's only the elders who say to the child, 'Don't do this, don't do that, don't play with this...' All the judgements that are brought in a child by the adults are the biggest disservice done to them. So, let's try and get rid of all these preconceived ideas which work as negative filters in receiving the gift that the present moment brings to us. Let us not lose the power of the present moment. This moment brings us the opportunity to either be in bliss or to be stuck in the past and the concerns about the future. The choice is ours. Let us choose wisely.

CHAPTER 23: GURUDEVA, INNER GURU

Today is day 23 of our *Parayanam,* and it also coincides with my Master, Sri Sathya Sai Baba's birthday. How do we celebrate the birthday of that entity which encompasses the creative life force? The ode to any Master or *Guru* is when we live their message in our lives and become their messengers. The reason I chose to become a messenger was because His message had a miraculous effect on my life. We've all had our own experiences with Baba. We all say that Sri Sathya Sai Baba was a man of miracles. Each one of us has a different understanding of what a miracle means. To some, He had the power to heal and bring back the dead to life. To others, He could make the lame walk, the blind see, the dumb talk and the deaf hear. He could materialise the entire range of jewellery, ornaments and idols. He could even manifest living beings like monkeys! Just waving His hand, he would produce objects at will, and the one which He gave away to everyone was the sacred ash (*Vibhuti*), which has the ability to heal and cure. It was also a reminder to everyone that, ultimately, the truth of the body is the ashes which we will finally become.

However, to me, the biggest miracle of Baba was my own transformation. I cannot speak about anyone else but me. He picked me at a late stage, sometime in 2007, just four years before He left His physical body. Because of His grace and love for me, He completely changed my life, without much conversation other than some eight or nine sentences in all those four years. Everything else just happened in His presence, in His being. From who I was then to what I am today seems like having lived four or five lifetimes, in what was a roller-coaster journey that started with my first contact with the Divine Master.

What I loved about Baba was the simplicity of His message, His ability to say the most complex thing in the simplest of ways, and the love that we experienced in His physical presence. We would not mind those long hours sitting cross legged on the floor, waiting for His arrival knowing there was not going to be any conversation, yet there was some magic that would transpire. Looking back at my journey, there are some things I have picked up that I want to share with everyone.

The first one is His message that we are all embodiments of love and divinity. He started every talk by addressing us as embodiments of love and divinity. Such is the human mind that there are some things that are very nice to hear but fall on deaf ears. We love to hear them, but we nonchalantly disregard them as if we had never listened to them. I do not know whether we can truly say that we believe the Master or *Guru*. One thing that I did was to completely take my time. I took a year to transform my belief into faith. Having tested Him, I did not doubt a single word of His, though he said very little to me. He just told me one thing, which He kept repeating through every dream I had of Him: 'You and I are one'. Actually, He never gave me any other messages! It must be His grace that a monkey mind like mine completely trusted him! I had faith in those words. I loved Him so immensely that I never called myself a devotee. I always called myself His lover, and I knew He reciprocated that love. In this love and oneness, I not only found myself but I found everything.

Actually, His whole message, and that of all the Masters, is only one of love and oneness. That physical *Guru* which we saw soon became the 'Inner *Guru*' or '*Gurudeva*', who got installed in the heart. The formless Principle took a human form which we called the *Kali Yuga Avatar*. Throughout His life, He gave thousands of discourses, but every discourse had just one essence: 'I am God and you are God. The only difference is that I know it and you do not. I have come to make you realise that you are also God'.

In the Bhagavad Gita, Krishna says,

'Yada yada hi dharmasya glanirbhavati bharata
Abhythanamadharmasya tadatmanam
srijamyaham'

Every time that *Dharma* falls, an Avatar comes to protect the good people who are following *Dharma* and to annihilate the *Adharmic.* He comes to protect what is moral and ethical in society. But, to my mind, what He comes for is to show man a mirror, the true reflection of his own Self, and to take him on the path of liberation. For this, Baba made the ultimate sacrifice of leaving His body ten years before the term He had declared, because He wanted to demonstrate to us that the Self or *Atman* is not the body; it is the energetic principle, the Consciousness that we have been talking about. He shed His body, which lay for three days in Puttaparthi. I was present there, sitting next to it for three days, knowing fully well in my heart that this body was not my *Guru.* The message that came to me then was, 'I am not he, I am thee'.

Soon, I experienced the presence of my Master with me all the time. I realised that my mind had always played with me telling me that my *Guru* was in Puttaparthi, so I kept running after Him. All running stopped and the experiences of His presence started to deepen. I realised that the body was a myth, because He was still present. Within three months of this, all of a sudden my father passed away and I started to experience the same principle of the presence of my father. Now, I had two fathers: one *Guru* and this body's father! I could access both because Baba had given me this experience that, while the body goes, the spirit or energetic presence (*Atman*), remains. It is an intelligence, a super Consciousness and one can interact with it. Hence, I also started to experience oneness with Him.

Those lessons were going to be further instilled in me

when, after five years, my wife suddenly merged with Baba. Then, I realised for a fact that the body was just an appearance, an illusion. It is what we get attracted and attached to, but the principle does not go away and we can tap and interact with it. In another two years, God chose that it was not enough and my mother also passed away. By this time, I had experienced death at close quarters and I realised that it was an illusion. Actually, death is a celebration because all the disabilities or shortcomings that a body has are overcome when we become bodiless and the phenomenon of being ever present is suddenly experienced.

Baba was not done with leaving the body. He said, 'I am going to make all of you realise that, like Me, you are God.' So, in these intervening ten years, he picked up a boy who was His student, whose name was Madhusudan. He trained him to be His communicator and then He trained him to start accessing bits and pieces of that Consciousness till he was fully ready to be able to hold that Divine Consciousness or realise his own Self. He created an example for each one of us, that a human being can also ascend to Divine Consciousness. We cannot say that only a Divine Being descends into a human form. A human being can also experience Self-realisation and experience that same Consciousness which is present in all of us. We sometimes experience Consciousness as synchronicities through connectedness.

The common thing between the journey of Madhusudan Sai and my own is that both of us believed in our Master. My Master told me what I will be doing in the future and said, 'I am giving you a gift that all you need to know is known by you, because I am one with you.' I never doubted it. I completely believed in my Master and everything started to happen. The faith which we sometimes lack is the reason why we are not able to progress rapidly on this journey. When we say we are hoping to do something, we are already creating doubts in our mind as we are not sure; and when we are not sure nothing ever happens. However, if we believe in the truth of the words of our *Guru* or our Master and put them into practice, then those words have the power to redeem us, even in that instant, because the present moment is all there is. It is a gift of Consciousness to us. If we are fully aware and fully focused, we can redeem ourselves and realise our divinity in this instant.

We all are on this journey together. Everybody is part of this divine drama that leads us to experiencing who we truly are. There is an unlimited source of power, energy, creativity and creation inside of us but we are unable to fathom it because our mind is holding us back. We are not able to comprehend that we are divine, that we are the God to whom we have been praying.

This is where faith is essential because, if we cannot comprehend, then at least we can rely on someone who can, who has seen and experienced his divinity. Baba has spoken endlessly about this, both in the physical form and in the subtle form travelling to various countries. We have thousands of His talks, now captured in the Uvacha and other series and translated into various languages. Yet, nobody opens them. We translate them, we keep them, we do all the *Seva,* listen to every talk and want to be in His physical presence, but we don't do *Manana.* Really, even one talk is enough. If we choose to start practising, even one experience is enough to transform us. However, if we allow doubts to come in it means we are really not so serious and are not going within. Whether it is an issue of lack of faith, lack of *Manana* or of *Nididhyasana,* we are still not able to overcome the mind.

The message of the *Guru,* whose ninety-seventh Birthday we are celebrating today was the message of our divinity because His message of 'Love all, Serve all' cannot be put into practice until we know what love is, until we know that that love which is the creative life force, is God, is the *Guru,* is the inner *Guru,* is the *Atman* inside of us and that we are the embodiments of love. When we experience the true love that is within us -not this bodily love which is only attachment and causes pain and suffering-, it starts to flow and ooze out of us from every pore of our skin, cells and hair, e.g. like the love that Hanuman had for Rama. That love is the essential nature of every being.

Baba would keep calling us *Premaswaroopalara*, embodiments of divine love. That is the gift He has given to all of us. I chose to receive it because I believed in my Master. If you too believe in your Master and in His message, and if you too believe that this is who you are, and if you keep this in your awareness all the time, that this is your truth and not what your mind keeps prompting you, and if you remain in this, it will become your reality. *'Brahmavid brahmaiva bhavati* – the knower of *Brahman* is verily *Brahman.'* That is when we start to love all.

We can't take coaching classes on how to love. Love is the only thing that happens naturally and spontaneously. A mother loves her child naturally. When we see an animal, we immediately start petting it. When we see beauty around in nature, love comes out. Love cannot be practised. It is spontaneous. That means it is inside of us. Our problem is that we start to get attached and feel we own the object of our love and hence we get into troubled waters. We were meant to love because love is who we are, love is all there is. We just came to experience this love, but we got entangled when the mind came in. It wanted to own, control and manipulate. It turned into jealousy and started to do funny things. So, when we experience the Truth, the presence of Baba in us, the presence of all those loved ones who were in a body once, then we experience the love that flows out to everyone, knowing that the same love is within everyone. So, when we love ourselves, then only we can love all because once we love ourselves and we know what love is, then that love cannot be curtailed. It just flows. Baba always said, 'Love is expansion'.

When we love everyone as ourselves, there is no question

of serving anyone. Service means we are doing something for somebody else, and as we do not serve our own selves we do not serve someone else but will be doing all that we need to do because we see the same Self in everybody. This will come naturally to us.

To me, this is the essential message of Sri Sathya Sai Baba. It is the same message being spread by Sadguru Madhusudan Sai. It is the same message that I bring because there is no other message. And the best way of celebrating the birthday of any *Guru* is to follow the path which He has laid for us. I walked on it, I am still walking on it and will continue to do so. I experience a deep sense of peace and complete detachment from all that used to be very dear to me.

That is the message of love, faith and miracle I wanted to share today, because the outer miracles are not real miracles. The real miracle is the transformation of the heart, from human to divine. May Baba's love flow through our hearts forever. May we let go of anything and everything that we have been holding on to, and may we experience oneness with Him. May we experience that love which is not outside us but within us. This is who we are. Let us experience the divine love of Mother Sai as we wish Him a very happy birthday. May His blessings be received by everyone. Thank you, Baba, for Your blessings and Your love. We fully believe in You. We are completely committed to experiencing our divine Truth.

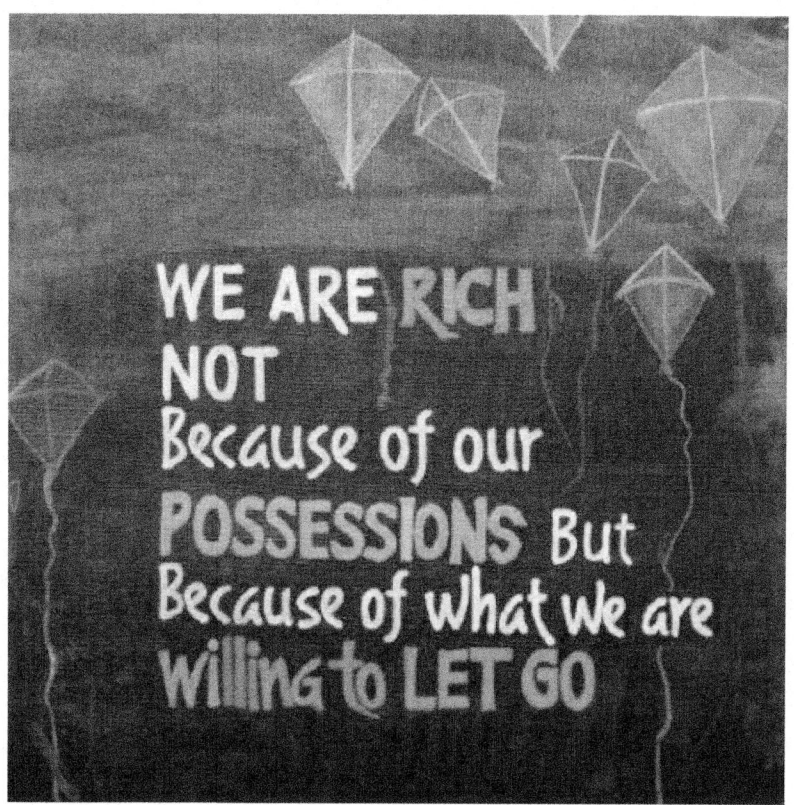

CHAPTER 24: VAIRAGYA OR DETACHMENT

Welcome to day twenty-four. Yesterday we celebrated the Birthday of our *Guru*, our *Gurudeva*, as both our outer *Guru* and inner *Guru*. We remembered His message and concluded that the real tribute to a *Guru* is not to fall at His feet or run after Him, but to follow His message and become a living embodiment of it. We also spoke about the form and the formless.

The day before, we had spoken about accepting and living in the present moment, since life is uncertain. Death can come any moment unannounced. Therefore, knowing the certainty of death, knowing we come empty handed and go empty handed, knowing all relationships are left behind, we must then understand that the way to the goal of life is the path of detachment.

Today, we will be talking about this detachment. We are all attached to the body of our loved one(s) when there is life and there is consciousness in it; but as soon as the consciousness leaves, the same body of our loved one becomes a stranger. Such a stark reality must make us contemplate and reflect upon the impermanence of life, its fickleness and how overly invested we are in our relationships and properties we hold on to and get bound to. Anything that fixates us or that we get attached to is a cause of great joy and sorrow at the same time, because attachment creates expectations and, where there is an expectation, disappointment is waiting round the corner to greet us.

Who are these people to whom we are so attached? Why are we attached? Is it because they are our blood relatives? Why do we call those with whom we are in a conjugal relationship as our very own? Till we met them, we did not even know where they were born and which family they belonged to. Yet, because we stay together and start depending on each other, we start getting attached, knowing fully well that one day, the *hamsa* (swan) will fly alone. There is a popular song composed by Kabir Das ji which says, '*ud jayega hans akela, jag darshan ka mela*', which means that the *hans* - swan (individual soul), which lives inseparably with its mate when it's alive, will (have to) fly alone at the time of death (no one goes with the dead to the world beyond); so, consider this world to be a temporary place (like a town fair with all its attractions) and live in it unattached. Usually, a pair of swans are always together and move together in unison as one. That is why, when we see a perfect couple always together, doing things together, we say that they are like a pair of swans. We simply cannot think of being able to live without our partners, knowing well that when the moment comes, one of them will have to fly alone. Knowing the finality of this, yet we do not use this to build detachment in us. We will grieve at our loss, and then after some time, we will only remember them on their anniversaries and birthdays. Slowly, they will start to fade from our memories.

Imagine how many lifetimes we've had these relationships with countless numbers of people! With some we worked, with others we played, with some we were friends or siblings and to some we were married. Where are those relationships now? We do not even know or have any memory of them. So, we must understand that everything in this world, this *Jagat,* is temporary. This body too is temporary and is set to leave at some point of time unknown to us. So, why don't we prepare ourselves in such a way that we learn the art of detachment? It is like climate change. We know about it but are not doing anything to arrest climate change; we talk about it, protest about it and then lament when people die. It is the same with the subject of dying and death - be it our death or our loved ones'. Perhaps we keep away these thoughts so that we do not have to accept impermanence. We must understand this impermanence, get into relationships without attachment and learn to enjoy them, for everything created in this universe is for our enjoyment. The Isha Upanishad says,

īśāvāsyam idam sarvaṁ
yat kiñca jagatyāṁ jagat
tena tyaktena bhuñjīthā
mā gṛdhaḥ kasya svid dhanam

God is prevalent everywhere. In everything and in every atom, God Consciousness pervades. All that is available in nature is for man's enjoyment, but man has to understand how to enjoy it. What is the technique given by the Isha Upanishad for enjoyment? It says, 'Enjoy with a sense of self-sacrifice'. Enjoy everything but with the outlook of sharing with others, not trying to own, hoard and keep things for ourselves. It also says that we should not have an eye on the wealth and property of others, and that we should only hold on to that which is essential for us and share the rest.

The first *Guru* of the Sikhs, Guru Nanak Devji, taught that we should work hard, *Kirat karo,* and that we should only eat after sharing with others, *Vand chhako,* because the same Self exists in them as well. We can learn the beautiful art of enjoying everything without trying to cling on to those things. In our relationships, we cling on to people like weeds cling to us when we climb a mountain. The weeds cling for the sake of pollination, but we cling to find our happiness mistaking it to be in them, rather than within our own Self. This tendency of developing hooks (attachments) and clinging on to people or things needs correction.

If we look around, we find that some people are very attached to their homes, so much so that they do not even go on holidays. They want to be in their own homes all the time. There are some devotees who have apartments here in the *Ashram* where I stay but they do not allow their apartments to be used by anybody else, when they are not staying here even though they seldom come. That is the amount of possessiveness that we have to things. Having such attachments, how can one follow the path of 'Love All Serve All'? These are nothing but examples of attachment of how we are not able to let go of what we think is ours. Attachment is not only to people, properties and things, but also to ideas and beliefs. Given below are some examples:

- We want things done in a certain way.
- We want to force our ideas on the people around us.
- We have a fixed way of thinking and our own world view, so anything that comes in the way throws us out of balance.
- We cannot accept the views of others and end up criticising or judging   them.
- We become 'cultish' in our approach.

We all know that we are free Consciousness. This truth of who we are, the *Atma,* the Consciousness, that is inside of us, is beyond any kind of label given to the body, the mind or any relationship. So, whatever strong viewpoint we hold about something, we should find them out and examine by asking within, 'What are these strong thoughts, ideas, relationships and objects that I am attached to?'

A lot of people on this path of detachment give up their properties, their homes, and their loved ones and walk into the forest, but that alone does not make us detached. It is in fact running away! Such people are not able to leave their thoughts behind. Whether they are in a forest or on a mountain, their thoughts become nightmares since they are not able to overcome them. Detachment does not mean giving up what we have, running away from people we love, giving up our properties or not having opinions or ideas. It means being ready to accommodate and to let go as and when the time demands. Our happiness should not depend on either having or not having those relationships and objects. We should be neutral, knowing the finality of it all.

Detachment also means being flexible with our ideas, so that there is room for others to co-exist with us, however difficult or different it might be. Remember, we are living in a world of polarities and contradictions, where duality is all around us, where opposing forces are always at play. Our attachments give birth to strong viewpoints and these viewpoints make us unhappy. Once we understand this clearly, we start becoming flexible. This is a step towards withdrawal or detachment.

I will give you an interesting example. I learnt this long back from my uncle, who was in the army. One day he told me, 'In the army, we are taught the art of advancement as well as the art of withdrawal. Every time a unit of the regiment has to move from one place to another, a forward party goes first to identify the next place, set up a forward camp, stay there for a while, complete their search and once satisfied the entire unit moves to the new forward base. They remain in their new base for a specified period and keep doing their engagement exercises to show their presence to the enemy. Then, when there is no longer a need to engage with the enemy, we do a systematic withdrawal'.

When my uncle shared with me this idea of withdrawal, I thought it was something important. How to lead and how to go forward is easy because we are full of enthusiasm; but sometimes we become very careless or hasty when we do our withdrawal, and sometimes we continue to remain engaged. I started thinking that, in life, ever since we are born, we have only learnt how to engage and do a forward advancement. We have engaged with different relationships, be it friends or family. The families keep growing in size, with the arrival of children and grandchildren. We are constantly engaging more and more with life, getting engrossed and attached. We do not know how to do a systematic withdrawal, because we don't realise that one day we will have to go back to the home from where we came. Home is not the place where we are living right now, but the place from where we have come. So, if we know that we have to return there, shouldn't we also know how to withdraw and prepare to go back? All our life we have been like a bull, charging forward and forward, but no one has told us, 'Ok, it's time now, let's start to withdraw!'

How do we start to disengage, detach and withdraw? How do we withdraw back these five senses which have become like tentacles, keeping us hooked and attached to various things, objects and people? How do we pull back from all those things that look so pretty and attractive? How do we withdraw, so that the only thing that we like is the sound of sacred music, the chanting of the name of God or *Satsanga*? We must start withdrawing, rather than waiting for things to be forced on us. I call it systematic withdrawal. Unless we detach, our mind will always overwhelm us, as it works on attachment.

During our meditations, when we expect results in a certain way, know that it is also due to our attachment to the result. It is the mind that steps in because our detachment is not fully complete so we are unable to hear the language of the energetic life force. A necessary condition for that is our detachment from the world. When we like to be silent, we even find sound to be violent to our ears and we gradually start enjoying being by ourselves. It is an indication of detachment, and it happens when the Consciousness within us starts to awaken. Our Upanishads have spoken about how *Vairagya* (detachment) starts coming and we lose interest in all the things after which we used to run. We ran after playthings when we were small. We ran after women when we were young. We ran after material things, be it a house or a car, when we became older. Then, slowly, we start to realise that all of life has gone outwards into acquiring things, getting attached to them and trying to maintain them. But the real Self, the real peace that we are looking for is not outside of us but inside.

We know fully well that all these relationships are ephemeral, temporary and can go in an instant. These are wake up calls, reminders of the truth of the reality of life. We must understand that this is a rule and a law of life. When the time is right, the soul will exit because it is all perfectly ordained. So, when the time is already set and when it is surely going to happen, why are we scared about it? Why are we attached to anything? No matter what we do, our tenure here cannot be extended; no matter what our blunders are, it cannot get reduced. It is going to happen at the right time and it is inevitable. Then why not live like a king or a queen in this present moment, enjoying to the fullest? Why get bound by unnecessary thoughts in the mind?

I enjoy being a parent and having my relationship with my children because I am completely detached. I have very little expectations from them. And yet, whatever needs to be done, I do. Detachment does not mean 'no attachment'. Detachment does not mean running away from your responsibilities and duties. Instead, detachment means no expectations. It allows us to enjoy everything much more than when we are attached. The emotion, the thought goes away and what remains is only the natural state of who we are, which is Ananda (bliss). Attachment is like the chain on our ankles which is tying us down to a heavy stake. It does not let us move freely around, like Consciousness does. It is our mind which brings attachment.

Today, we are discussing that detachment is the key, and also how it is a challenge for us. It does not mean that we do not enjoy what God has provided us with, either family or possessions. It means creating a balance, moving away from expectations, from all that brings fear or hurt to our life, making us freer to do what we need to do. The path becomes easier to traverse. We instantly start feeling lighter, as if somebody has lifted a big load from us.

Yogic Technique for Inner Cleansing

One of the most powerful techniques to deal with attachments is called the *Trikuti.* which means a triangle of three equal sides. Just above our third eye, there is an equilateral triangle where the *Guru chakra* or the *Trikuti* lies. Invoking the grace of the *Guru*, we can light the fire of knowledge there. It is the highest of all the fires, and it has the ability to cleanse all emotions, attachments, thoughts and ideas that bind us. It is the only fire that does not burn, but cleanses. Sit in silence, in a meditative posture, focus on your third eye and ask your *Guru* or your family deity to help you to ignite the *Trikuti* right above your third eye. Once this light is lit, bring to the *Trikuti* whatever thoughts, attachments, relationships and emotions bother you and offer those thoughts or emotions to the fire. As you do so, you can say a small prayer. Now you have handed it to the fire of knowledge, and this knowledge will cleanse the emotion and remove the ties that are binding you.

It is a very powerful yogic technique. There may be many thoughts in your subconscious which are deep seated and which you do not remember but are troubling you. You can actually pray to your subconscious and to your *Guru* to help you access all those things that you do not even remember. It brings to the fore incidents that may have happened in your childhood which you don't even remember. However, the subconscious stores everything. Suddenly you will remember something and wonder where it has come from. Whatever thoughts come, keep offering them into this fire.

It is a very strong exercise and, when you do it, you will experience a lot of heat on your forehead. You will also sweat and feel an energetic release ensuing from your body, because every thought has an energy, everything is an energy. It may take you a couple of hours or a couple of days, because we have been storing things inside of us for God knows how long. Therefore, keep cleaning and cleaning and it should be able to help you.

Note: Please refer to the Appendix section for information on practicing the Trikiuti technique.

CHAPTER 25: VIVEKA OR DISCRIMINATION

Welcome to day twenty-five of the *Atma Chalisa Parayanam*. We spoke about detachment and realised how most of our challenges lie with our attachments. We saw how the mind entangles itself through attachments to people, things, objects, places, time, ideas and opinions. The whole idea of 'mine' and 'thine' comes with this attachment. It is the root cause of our unhappiness, sorrow, suffering and the chatter in our mind. This trap of expectations that comes from our attachments starts to complicate things in our lives. We are unable to do what needs to be done because of either looking at the results or our expectations or at the expectations of others from us. This is a big trap and it makes us take actions which, instead of helping us or others, end up creating more confusion, entanglements and challenges. The expectations that others have from us sometimes make us say or do things we don't really want, not to displease them. This is when the entanglements or knots start in our life.

We realise that making people happy by meeting their expectations is the most thankless thing to do and will never be fulfilling for anyone. Then we begin to realise that these attachments arise from the lack of understanding our own Self and, in the same light, from the lack of understanding of the ones whom we are attached to. As I mentioned, we might look at our own selves differently but we do not allow this luxury when we view others, because we are mostly playing the victim card for ourselves. Either we have to fight for things, force others or succumb to others. So, something or the other we create in our minds; but, the challenges are coming from our attachments, born out of our false idea of what love means.

When we detach, it gives rise to discrimination or discernment. Discrimination does not mean discriminating between people; on the contrary, it means we start to discriminate about what is right and what is wrong. This helps us to perform our duties and responsibilities properly towards our loved ones, the members of the society and Mother Nature. There are many examples in our daily lives, like that of a mother and her child. Sometimes, a mother is able to discern that a particular thing is not good for the child and, even if the child is unhappy, she doesn't succumb to its demands or desires and holds firm. However, many times we are unable to do that. Our attachments are so strong that we succumb to them. We give in just to please others, knowing inside of us that it is not right. Yet, because of our attachment and the expectations from others, we end up doing those things. In the bargain, we are unhappy and dissatisfied.

Discrimination is the capacity to do what is right, to do what we must do to discharge duly our duties or responsibilities in life. None of us can run away from discharging our duties. No matter what stage of life we are in or what our social status is, we are always engaged in the performance of our duties to our families, our societies, the world at large and Mother Nature. There is no running away from it. But how do we do this skilfully and perfectly, in a way that gives us that inner joy we are looking for, without having to compromise, get deterred by consequences or give in to please someone? This is where discrimination helps us - to discern how to do what we have to do in the best possible way. Our Upanishads and the whole of Vedanta philosophy say that two angels walk with us on our journey towards Self-realisation, *Viveka* and *Vairagya*. *Viveka* is the ability to discriminate and discern, whilst *Vairagya* is detachment. Both feed each other.

It is clear that, when we start detaching by accepting and letting go, we are able to see things much more clearly, as then our discriminative capacity is not muddled or clouded by our emotions, beliefs, ideas and experiences. We are able to see things as they are. Discrimination is the ability to see things as they are and then perform the actions that are in the best interest of everyone. These two angels go hand in hand, constantly taking us towards our goal of abiding in the Self, in the zone of one Consciousness. Every time a situation comes and we are able to see it for what it is, without judging, clouding it, imagining it, without being overwhelmed by our senses and without giving in to the pressure of people around us, that intellect or the ability to discriminate takes us rapidly towards our goal. This is because we are able to see things and deal with them very effectively. As we keep doing this, the detachment grows more and more. As the detachment grows, the discriminative capacity also grows stronger, because both of them are deeply connected. They are like best buddies who always operate together.

A sense of balance starts coming when we start to practise discrimination and detachment in our daily life. That is when systematic withdrawal comes in; this feeling of wanting to be on our own rather than with people. Detachment is freeing up time which we have spent engaging with people outside. That time is now available for us to look at things in perspective, without running to fulfil the desires of others and being under pressure and anxiety about how to fulfil their expectations. In trying to please others, we end up not pleasing ourselves and becoming exhausted.

We must know that the only way we can make others happy is not by fulfilling their expectations, but by spreading the joy which is within us and sharing it with everybody. It is by loving everyone and serving everyone. But for that, first we must know ourselves. As Shirdi Baba said, 'When we know our own Self, then we know everybody else.' *Aham Brahma, Sarvam Brahma.* God knows us because He knows Himself.

The path of being joyous and creating joy for others is not a path of confrontation, it is not the path of trying to fulfil the expectations of others, but the path of experiencing withing us the joy of who we truly are. Then it will spread to everyone else.

The Upanishads say that the primary duty of every human being is *Atmano mokshartham jagat hitaya cha*-realisation of our true Self and service to the society. If we experience Self-realisation, free ourselves from the pulls and pressures of this illusory world, understand that everyone else is also divine and has come for hisown mission in this birth, our perspective of life totally changes. For example, we begin to understand that our children do not eternally belong to us, they are but eternal souls on a mission, who have had different sets of parents and different sets of relationships in their past lifetimes.

So, when we start discriminating who we truly are and apply the same principle to the people around us, suddenly something loosens and we are able to look at the challenges in a very detached way, knowing that we have been giving too much of self-importance to ourselves as if the whole world depended on us. Once that understanding of our own selves comes in, everything starts to dissolve by itself. Hence, instead of trying to make everyone else happy and putting out every fire around us, let us fulfil the most basic urge of every human being, which is to find that source of eternal peace and bliss within us.

As soon as we do that, everything else falls into place. It is like a masterstroke. We put the centrepiece of the jigsaw puzzle and all other pieces around start to fit. It is so beautiful. As soon as we are happy and as soon as we are peaceful, the world starts to appear so peaceful and loving. We stop looking at the challenges of the world and start looking at all the joys that are available, because that is what we are feeling inside. *Yad bhavam tad bhavati;* as we feel, that is what we manifest in the world. We are just a projection. Remember the white screen we are constantly projecting on? If we cannot stop projecting, then at least let us project happiness and joy, coming not from outer things that are going to fade away but from deep inside of us. This joy comes from our beingness. It is who we are, when we are not on guard or putting on a show. It is a natural feeling.

Thus, discrimination and detachment are those two angels which are constantly leading us towards our goal. The silence that comes from detachment, from going within, makes our ability to discern blossom. We start seeing errors that we have been making. We are able to make corrections. We start to see our ego, our weaknesses. We start to see that people are nothing but a reaction, reflection and resound of us. They are mirrors that are trying to show us something. That ability to see things as they are, without colouring them with our mindset, is ultimately going to help us to become the observer, the *Drashta*, the witness. We are able to see everything going on around us without reacting, just observing. The world that gets projected outside including the so-called family, the so called-society, is a part of the apparent reality which is illusory. Since our own existence is not this body, so the existence of the people we are seeing is also not the body. There is something inside of us, inside each one of us, which is who we truly are. It is permanent, eternal, divine.

During this *Parayanam*, the ability to discern and detach, without reacting instantly from the mind, has been growing in each one of us. As things become clearer to us, we experience a change. Once we stop responding to the urges of the mind, something happens within us and our focus starts to shift from the outward to the inward. So, the twins (*Viveka* and *Vairagya*) are already at work within each one of us which we can appreciate when we silently reflect upon our journey so far.

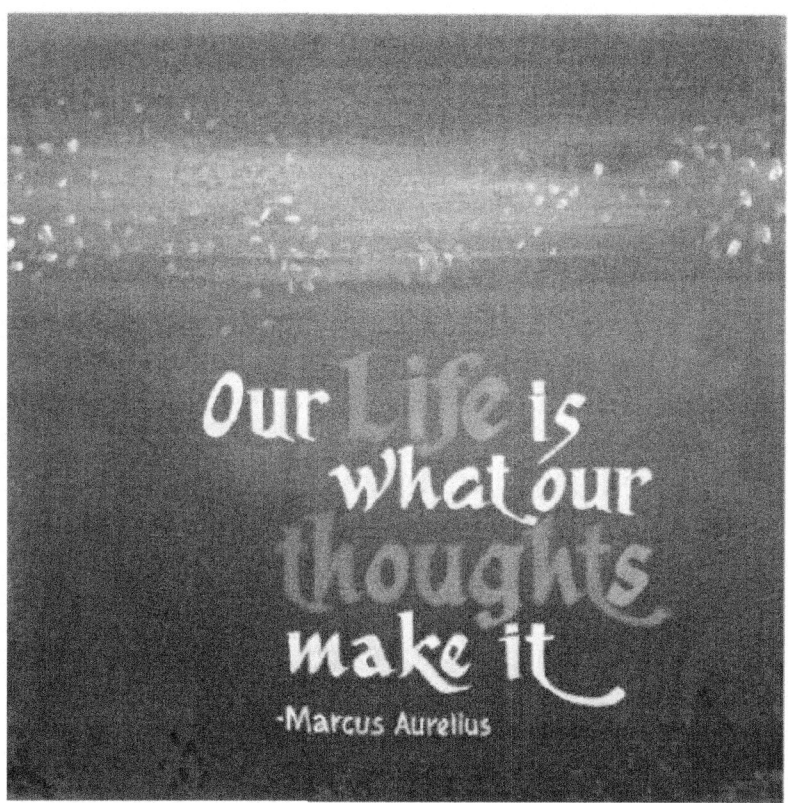

CHAPTER 26: LIFE IS A GAME

Today, we will talk about the idea of 'Why life is a game, and why we should actually take it as a game'. I think it is very important to understand this as well as experience it too. Otherwise, we will tend to make life appear too heavy, which brings pain, stress and anxiety. When I hear some saying that to detach is difficult, when I see we sometimes get uncomfortable in certain situations and start thinking anxiously about certain events in the future, all this points to the fact that we are taking life too seriously. Because we do this, we build stakes on this life as if our life depended on it. But what is life and what is this dependency?

We must examine all these things to realise how funny life is. Actually, it's all about contradictions: experiencing heat as well as cold, finding joy when everybody is finding things difficult, finding humour in life when things are absolutely crazy around us. By now, all of us know that the only certainty in life is that we are going to die. There is no suspense to it, only the timing is unknown. The body is impermanent. Nothing is going to last and we are not going to take anything back with us, neither the objects nor the people who are around us. They're just associated with us. In fact, the day when we come and the date of our exit are already fixed. Then, what are we serious about in life?

Those things we think we're going to lose and those things we think we're going to gain, those things that we desire, those things that we never got and all those people around with which we are trying to build this whole castle of life, nothing is going to last. Then, where is the question of having any stakes in life? When we know that life is such a play, we must discover and experience that which is not going to die, that which is beyond birth and death, that which is permanent and immortal, before this body becomes feeble and too old to respond. It is a treasure hunt! Have we ever cried or felt stressed in a treasure hunt? Have we ever felt any kind of unhappiness or negativity? It's such a beautiful game! We're searching, we're looking at clues and we're trying to decipher those clues. We're trying to figure things out with great excitement and joy. There is no sense of remorse of having played in a treasure hunt.

In this game of life, the duration of which is uncertain, we are on a treasure hunt. How beautiful is this game! How beautiful is this setting! All that we have is this present moment. How amazing is this play, this *Maya* (where the unreal appears to be real) that God or the Universal Consciousness has created! Krishna calls it a *Leela*, a sport. How amazing that we find it so real! How amazing that we fall into it when our five senses make us go astray! But that's what the game is. We understand the foolishness of how we fell into it as we awaken, as we start understanding, as the light of knowledge comes. *Asato Ma Sad Gamaya Tamaso Ma Jyotir Gamaya...* - the prayer says, 'O, Universal Consciousness, please take me from the unreal to the real; remove the ignorance by bringing the light of knowledge in my life, so that I experience the immortal Truth and my attachment to this false idea that I am the body and the doer falls away forever'. Just imagine how beautiful and how simple it is!

When this understanding comes to us, in an instant we can shake off all that is unreal. But we keep insisting on how difficult it is and how hard we are trying. What do we mean by trying? Either we believe in Truth or we don't. If we believe in it, where is the question of trying? When we say that we're trying, it means we are not doing anything. It means that we are not convinced about it, or that we are too weak to put it into practice. We must remember that the only way to experience something in life is to do *Shravana, Manana* and *Nididhyasana*. And *Nididhyasana* (practice) does not happen if we have not done enough reflection or *Manana* (contemplation). We have not convinced ourselves that, where is the question of attachment if we are divine souls, if we are the Supreme Consciousness, and so is everybody else? Where is the question of good and bad, ugly and evil, danger, fear or desires? But since we just pick up one thought and look at it in isolation, forgetting everything else, our desires and our attachments take over. That is why it is called *Maya*, and the only way to tackle this is to keep contemplating, till it gets completely focused in our head.

We are definitely not weak. Whatever we want to do we always end up doing. So, when we say, 'I'm unable to do this', it means we are not willing to do it. We still like the idea of holding on to our attachments. Everything else is an excuse, because what we really want, we just do it. We've had enough examples of that in our life and we know that's the truth. We're just hiding behind our attachments because, somehow, we like it. And that's the reason why we build stakes because we are always fearful about people; we are always fearful about things that may go wrong. Therefore, this life keeps tracking us and we are not able to experience that life is a game. It was never meant to be heavy. Remember that God created everything so that everyone could enjoy the beauty of His Creation. It was created out of sheer love, so that this love could be experienced by everyone. That is why we all came here on Earth.

We are all embodiments of the Divine. We've come here to experience love and discover that we are actually that source of love. But why has it become heavy? Why did the stakes become too high? Why are we so afraid? Why do we drag through life with such a heavy heart? It is because somewhere we started to develop hooks and get attached. 'Oh! I like this, let me have it. I like this, let me hold it for myself. I like this person, let me have this person in my life'. We just started to get attached to everything which we came to enjoy and love on this planet.

So, if we now understand that there lies our challenge,

then we will know exactly how to get out of it! The opposite of getting attached is to get detached, and what gives us the willpower to do it is the right understanding. What I am attached to is not real, it is illusory; and what is real and permanent is who we truly are! Life was never meant to be such a heavy place where the going got so difficult. The difficulty lies in this weakness of ours, born out of lack of knowledge. Therefore, now that we understand, we should be able to do something about it. There's no other way! We did things out of ignorance, because we did not understand what the goal of life was all about, why were there birth-death cycles. When we undo what we previously did, suddenly everything lifts up.

Previously, we introduced this powerful technique so beautifully explained by Swami Rama, the exercise of the *Guru chakra*, the *Jnana chakra* or the *Trikuti*, which helps us to cleanse our *Prarabdhas* (pre-destined due to our past Karmas), our *Vasanas* (innate tendencies), that have been troubling us. In an instant, all that has been holding us down starts to get cleared. Why is this information coming to us now? It's because we are seeking it. It's because our time has come. So, today I want to tell all of you to let go of this dread and doom, this fear and insecurity, this negativity, this idea of good, bad, ugly, likes and dislikes. This is the reason why we are in this world and are constantly getting trapped in it. We create a matrix around us and get trapped in that matrix, we've never been able to break through. In every life, we created more and more matrices and we kept building walls around us. In an instant, we can shatter all these walls. Once the kingpin or the centrepiece, which is the *Atman*, is in place, everything around starts to fall into place. That's what our journey is about, that is what we are trying to experience. We are trying to experience the Lord of the Universe that resides in us. We can call it *Gurudeva*, *Atman*, the Consciousness or any name that we like. The name just doesn't matter. It can only be experienced.

All those who are born, have to necessarily perform actions, duties, and fulfil responsibilities. We have been placed in different situations, families and circumstances according to which we must perform our *Dharma* (duty). We cannot escape from that, but we have a choice. Are we performing our actions with joy in our hearts or are we unhappy, approaching life with trepidation and fear in us? As soon as our perspective changes, as soon as we start seeing life as a game, a mission to be accomplished, things change. It is indeed a game, because there is nothing at stake. A stake is there when we are going to win or lose something. But in this game, where it's very clear that we came empty handed and we will go empty handed, there cannot be a stake. We can't even take our body along, forget anything else. The most rubbish thing which we are carrying and which keeps us in this cycle of birth and death is our mind. Right? So, all we have to do is to lose our minds. When we lose it, we don't become crazy. Instead, we gain something which is the essence of life.

Therefore, please spend this day fully integrating this understanding, and ruminating and reflecting on it. Be convinced. If not, then get all the doubts clarified. It doesn't take days, months and years to be who we really are. It can happen in an instant, once the understanding comes. If we are not convinced, then we must seek conviction; but if we are convinced, then there is absolutely no reason for us not to do what we need to do.

So, please take out the dread and the stake and bring joy back in life. See life as a game, because there is nothing to lose and yet everything to gain. What is it that we gain? We gain perpetuity. We taste the nectar of immortality. Once we have tasted it, we do not require to take a body again. It frees us from the eternal cycle of life and death and brings to us a state of perennial joy. We are released from these clutches. We are present in the moment, and we enjoy everything that comes. Challenges stop appearing to be challenges, they become situations. It's all a game.

When we play a game like monopoly, a situation comes to us, we laugh at it and we deal with it. We go into game shows or reality shows to enjoy them. There can't be a bigger reality show than life. Actually, there is an eternal witness within each one of us that is watching the entire game. As the Upanishads say, the observer is waiting for the actor to realise that there is a director, and that the director is within watching all the moves. We have to experience that the actor and the director are one. There never was an actor and there never was a director. It's just that they didn't recognise each other and kept thinking they were two.

So, to go around life as if it is painful clearly means that we've not understood it. Please, make all efforts to bridge the gap in the understanding if there is still any. I was a man on a mission, who said, 'I won't rest till I resolve this'. I've often given this example of a dog with a bone, who will not let go. It's just up to us. We have the power to actually shift everything in our consciousness. Life becomes joyous when we see everything as a game. As Baba used to say,' Life is a game, play it.' I say, 'Life is a game, play it and enjoy it.' Games are played only for entertainment. That's why people started to create entertainment, because otherwise they got bored. They found sports as an entertainment. They went into movies, dramas, theatres and music as entertainment. What if, actually, the whole of life is a game? What a sport! What joy! Then, suddenly, we start to attack the problems and challenges of life with gusto, with enthusiasm, with a song in our heart, with a spring in our step; and we dance along life with no worries.

I hope and pray that I've been able to transfer some of my enthusiasm, joy and love for life. My *Guru* told me to empty my pockets and to empty myself from all attachments. I realised this was such a beautiful advice that He had given me! Somebody asked me how it feels not having any of this. I said, 'Freedom, joy!' And yet, everything I need in life is beautifully arranged and there's only abundance. Remember always that as love starts to expand, it only brings abundance.

CHAPTER 27: THORN FOR A THORN

Welcome to day twenty-seven of the *Atma Chalisa Parayanam*. It is important to understand about life being a game and realising that all sorrow, pain and sufferings come from our attachments. That is what our mind specialises in. It keeps us hooked into this life and we come again and again, birth after birth, until one day we realise we've had enough and there must be something else to it. Once we detach, out of sheer exhaustion and frustration, we start to experience something profound. We start to feel a sense of freedom and lightness, because all the hooks and entanglements that were binding us down disappear. This lightness makes life joyful, for we receive whatever comes our way with enthusiasm, with a sense of adventure and excitement, knowing that it needs to be dealt with skilfully, because we've come here to hone our skills and bring perfection in the way we look at things and do things.

As soon as our attitude and perspective to life changes, something shifts inside of us. The heavy baggage that we are carrying, all the things that our mind makes a mountain out of, suddenly goes away. Anything that comes, for example a bad cold, we deal with it and just don't give it any importance. We don't get attached and it goes away. The more we think about something and focus on it, that grows. That is how thoughts hook us. Everything in life comes for a reason. We don't need to analyse the reason behind it going into past lives. It is all a game. The solution to a problem lies in the problem itself. Whenever someone asks me a question, I tell them that their answer is hidden in their question itself. All that is needed is *Manana* (contemplation) to arrive at the answer. When we sit with ourselves and do *Manana*, the question disappears because it was never there; it was the mind creating it. If we understand the mechanics of this body-mind duo and start operating from a higher consciousness, we will stop giving importance to these problems and they just fall away.

Let us now delve into Kathopanishad's wisdom, which we need to put into practice on our journey to Self -realisation, of using the concept of a thorn to remove another thorn that has pricked and got stuck in our flesh. We use another thorn to take out the one stuck in the flesh and then both thorns are discarded, the one that was embedded and the one we used to remove it.

There are two contexts associated with this concept. The first context is that of the mind. We are already acquainted with the lower mind and the higher mind. Higher mind is the pure intellect. It is the purified mind, which is subservient and under the control of consciousness. We need that higher mind to take out the lower mind which troubles us with desires, attachments and thoughts. After doing our *Manana,* when we want to put things into practice or *Nididhyasana,* if the lower mind is still troubling us with attachments, we will need the help of the higher mind to throw this thorn of attachment out of us.

In life, in order to take that last step forward, to move in, we need faith in the words of a Master, a *Guru* or a friend. The name by which we call him is unimportant, as long as we are receptive to learning from him. So, this faith will help us to remove that thorn. Thus a higher mind is essential to transcend the lower mind. When we take the decision to have faith and follow what is being taught to us, then that faith will bring us results, because the mind will see that there is a logic to follow. What is that logic to be followed? It is the promise of a guide who will take us on a journey that we are not sure of. The mind creates doubts and asks if we are going to be in trouble. But, when it understands that this guide is a skilled journey-man who knows the path, it starts to surrender. Slowly, the lower mind starts to merge with the higher mind and it becomes what we call a no-mind. It is very important to understand that, when we come to the point of doing or not doing, we still need the mind to say, 'Ok, let's do it'.

The second aspect which this first point leads us to is the role of the *Guru*. Where does the *Guru* step in? He steps in as a physical person once the seeker or disciple is ready, in order to fulfil the needs of the seeker (Refer Chapter 1). This role of the *Guru* keeps changing. Many *Gurus* may have come in our life. Dattatreya (the incarnation of the trinity Gods -Brahma, Vishnu and Shiva) had twenty-four *Gurus*! At any point of time, there is somebody who appears for what we need; but sometimes we become rigid and build up attachments to the physicality or essence of a particular *Guru*.

I will give a few examples from my own journey to explain this. When I started going to Puttaparthi to see Baba, I met a lot of devotees from all over the world. I heard their fascinating experiences and how they came in touch with Him. I found it odd that Baba would tell a lot of His devotees to go to a particular *Guru*. Many were sent to Maharishi Ramana, some to Swami Rama and some to a *Guru* ji in Vrindavan. I used to wonder why a *Param Guru* (Universal Teacher) like Sri Sathya Sai Baba, an Avatar, would send people to other *Gurus*. It was something that did not agree with me. But slowly, I started to experience that there was something more that needed to be acquired, and the Master knew what kind of teacher a particular seeker needed. It is like different subjects taught by different teachers. As the student advances in his or her studies, the principal of the University decides what a student requires and he or she is handed over from one teacher to another. I say all this from my personal experience.

As I told earlier, I used to follow Sri Shirdi Sai Baba and, almost for one full year, when I came in touch with Sri Sathya Sai Baba, I absolutely avoided Him. I used to go to a Sai Centre where there were two life size pictures of both Sri Shirdi Sai Baba and Sri Sathya Sai Baba on each side of the shrine. I remember that I used to only look at Shirdi Sai Baba's picture and not even look at Sri Sathya Sai Baba's, thinking, 'Oh, I don't want to be with this *Guru*, I already have a *Guru*. I'm very happy with Sri Shirdi Sai Baba'. Can you imagine? For one year I avoided looking at the picture of Sri Sathya Sai Baba. There was an adamancy in my heart. I was convinced that I did not need any other *Guru*; until, one day, Baba just caught hold of me and I found myself in Puttaparthi. After that, He became the breath of my life, the very essence of my existence, and I just could not think of being without Him. I soon realised how quickly I had moved from Sri Shirdi Sai Baba to Sri Sathya Sai Baba. Had He not pushed hard, I would have not come to His presence. Once there, I realised how the Master calls. We feel that it is our heart, but actually it is the mind that is so stubborn. It refuses to accept something which is right in front of us.

Thus, my romance, my immense love affair with Sri Sathya Sai Baba started and my life became beautiful. When people used to talk about other *Gurus*, *Mantras* (chants) and *Dikshas* (spiritual initiation), I just laughed at them and told them that we had a *mantra* called 'Love all, Serve all' and there was no need for any other *mantra*. Then, as the story of life goes on and you are led into situations, one fine day I read one of Swami Rama's books, 'Living with the Himalayan Masters'. This book and the 'Autobiography of a Yogi' have had a profound impact on me. Somehow, I related to Swami Rama as I saw a lot of similarities between us. Whenever I heard his talks on YouTube or read his books, I would feel, 'I am writing this or saying this'. I had a lot of love and regard for him.

In Noida, where I used to live, there was a very close devotee of Bhagawan Baba. She had the good fortune of having had more than a hundred interviews with Swami in Puttaparthi and Whitefield. She was sent by Baba to receive *diksha* from

Swami Rama. She was a great singer and we all adored her. At some point in her life, she got inspired to open a Centre of Swami Rama in Noida. Because I loved Swami Rama and because I loved her, I would often go to this Centre for *Bhajans* (collective singing of the glory of God) and various programmes. One of these times, when they were celebrating the first anniversary of the Centre, a Swami from Rishikesh was to come to give *diksha* to a number of people. There would be a *Satsanga* followed by *Prasadam* (blessed food).

Both me and my wife decided not to go, since we were not interested. The programme began at five in the evening and was to finish around eight. At about seven o'clock, I suddenly started to feel that we needed to go there. I suggested to my wife that we just go for the last half hour to keep everybody happy. We arrived at seven thirty at the Centre, when the Swami was conducting a meditation. We managed to find a place to sit and, as soon as I closed my eyes, Swami Rama was standing in front of me in a white robe. He slightly pulled his robe up and said, 'Take my *Padanamaskar*' (blessings received by touching the feet of a realised Master). I touched his feet and they felt absolutely real. Thereafter, he started to give me instructions on the purpose of life and, for the next twenty-five minutes or so, I was lost in this discussion with Swami Rama. Although not in his flesh and blood, he felt very real.

As soon as I opened my eyes, I saw that the mediation was over and everyone was going to meet the Swami, whilst I was just in this experience of mine, which was so profound. It had never happened to me before. I sat in a corner and did not want to meet anyone or share this with anyone, not even with my wife. About half an hour later, when everyone had met the Swami, the lady of whom I spoke about earlier called me and said, 'Why don't you come, meet Swami Ji and take his blessings?' There was no choice but to go. So, I called my wife and we both went to receive the blessings from the Swami. Then, he said, 'So, how was your experience?' I recounted to him exactly what had transpired and he immediately said, 'Oh the *Guru* has come, why don't you take *diksha*?' I instantly said, 'No, I do not want any *diksha*. I already have a *Guru*, Sri Sathya Sai Baba, and I don't want *diksha* from anyone else'.

He smiled and then looked towards my wife and asked her, 'How was your experience?' My wife said she had also seen Swami Rama standing in front of her and he kept telling her, 'Oh! My child, my daughter, please take *diksha*'. My wife was one who never spoke her mind and kept things to herself. For the first time in my living memory, I heard her say, 'Yes, I want *diksha*'. As we had never done things separately, I too agreed to take *diksha*!

The lady told us to come back the following morning at six thirty, after having a bath, and our *diksha* would be arranged. I said, 'I want my *diksha* right now. I am ready, and who knows if I will come back tomorrow'. She got very angry and upset with me and said, 'Are you stupid? There are rules and norms for giving *diksha*'. Before the argument could go any further, the Swamiji smiled and said, 'These two will get *diksha* now'. The lady protested saying that was not as per the norms, but he answered, 'Right now, no norms are going to be followed'.

So, at nine o'clock in the night, we were taken in for *diksha*. I was taken in first. The Swami said that whatever *Mantra* I would be getting, I should not disclose it to anyone ever, not even to my wife, since it was my own *Mantra*. I accepted. Then, I heard the voice of Swami Rama in my ears and a *Mantra* was given to me. The Swami explained the *Mantra* to me and then commented that everything that was happening was absolutely strange and fascinating. He said that, in the first place, I was the first initiate who had been given a *Mantra* in the night. The *Guru* was actually standing there and saying, 'Please give them *diksha* right now'. Secondly, he said that, in the Himalayan lineage, there are different *Mantras* for different levels of disciples. He added, 'It is the first time that an initiate (a first -time disciple) has been given the highest *Mantra* in our lineage and Swamiji came himself to give you the *Mantra*. I feel blessed that I am here performing this'.

I did not know what to make of it, except that some sort of blessing had taken us there. As you recall, I was stubbornly not wanting this, but thanks to my wife I got something which would soon change my life. Then, I was asked to leave and my wife was called in. Later, when I was called in again, I saw the Swami laughing and crying at the same time. He said, 'This is just incredible. Both of you have the same *Mantra*. For a couple to have the same Mantra is very rare; it has never happened in my tradition'.

The reason I am sharing this with you is that two times in my life I have been stubborn. Once, when it was about Sri Sathya Sai Baba, I didn't want to know Him, but I became his ardent disciple later on. Then, when I did not want a *Mantra* from a *Guru* whom I really loved, Swami Rama, I got the highest *Mantra* despite my unwillingness. So, many times in our lives, when something else is coming our way, we block it. This could be due to strong attachment or loyalty to our *Guru*. Whatever be the reason, there is something between the mind and the heart that happens which does not allow us to be fully present to the gifts that the Consciousness wants to give us in that particular moment. Thus, the attraction and attachment to our *Guru* itself becomes a thorn in us.

So, we must utilise the understanding of who the *Guru* truly is. Is the *Guru* a form? A *Guru* is associated with a form to start with, but the final understanding comes when another *Guru* in another body comes and helps us to install something far subtler inside of us and makes us experience that the *Guru* is actually only one. He comes in different forms at different times just to give us the message that we need at that moment. Many times, the message and messenger are right next to us and we keep blocking the messenger out because of some stubbornness in us. We are not able to perceive that it is the same *Guru* because the *Guru* will keep using different bodies, different forms and identities. Once we understand this, we must install the formless *Guru* inside of us because that *Guru*, after having taken various forms, becomes that formless Consciousness and is then available to us throughout our lives.

So, the *Guru* becomes *Gurudeva*. The *Guru* is the one with a form and the *Gurudeva* is the one that is worshipped inside of us. That *Gurudeva* is present all through our lives as one Supreme Consciousness. That Consciousness is a teacher, a guide and our own identity as well. There are subtle layers of experiencing that oneness. Until that merger is made, till that oneness is experienced at all times, until all stubbornness and all fixed ideas, notions, likes and dislikes, merge into this oneness, till that time, we will keep getting messages from the outside. We have to develop the ability to recognise the message and not the messenger and internalise it. Once we have internalised it, we experience eternal peace.

Once we have faith, first in the outer *Guru* and then in the inner *Guru*, this faith gives us the experience. We call it being in the state of knowingness. We start knowing; we always know. This knowingness ultimately becomes beingness. We are always in the state of 'being'. In this state, knowingness is also finished because knowingness came when we still had the faith that there was somebody else. Knowingness means that we know that things happen in a certain way guided by Consciousness. In the stage of beingness only one remains. We have merged with the *Guru* as one. All duality stops and that is what we've come to experience.

We have to use the higher mind to convince the lower mind to have faith; and that one act of faith can help the lower mind to surrender to the higher mind, which understands it is in safe hands and stops complaining! It stops to digress us from our path and is in consonance with the one Consciousness. Once this oneness comes, we experience peace and contentment.

This is required only once. So, remember the phrase from the Kathopanishad that we need a thorn to take out another thorn embedded in us and troubling us. Once we have removed both thorns, their use is over and no longer needed. That is why every good *Guru* distances himself or herself from the disciple when the disciple has finished receiving their wisdom. In that separation, we can experience that the *Guru* is not the body.

In his first message in 1940 at the age of fourteen, Sri Sathya Sai Baba said, 'I have come to light the lamp of love in your hearts so that it grows brightly'. Once the light of the lamp has been lit, and once the flame starts to grow, then we do not need the presence of another light. We are the light and that light then starts to remove the darkness from the path of many others on their journey.

CHAPTER 28: SAY YES TO LIFE

We spoke about the idea of removing the mind by using the mind, and removing the form of a *Guru* by using another *Guru* to move from the form to the Formless, from the *Guru* to the *Gurudeva*, the eternal Being that is always present. It does not mean that, when we get connected to the Universal *Guru*, to the omnipresent omniscient One, our connection with the physical *Guru* ceases. It means that the *Guru* is ever-present in our hearts guiding us. Therefore, there is no need of running after the physical form of a *Guru*, seeking advice and answers to our problems.

We will always remain eternally grateful to all the *Gurus*, masters and teachers who came into our lives and contributed significantly to our current state of experiencing the Consciousness. No words of gratitude are enough to pay our respects to all the masters who have been guiding us in our life. Now, as we are doing this final journey of experiencing the presence of the *Guru* within us, who will remove the darkness of ignorance and bring the knowledge of wisdom which will give us the experience of our divine nature, of the love that flows, that experience will guide and take over.

Whenever we happen to be in the physical presence of the *Guru*, our love, devotion and gratitude for him or her shall always remain. The only thing that changes is the hankering and running behind a physical form. For that reason, the *Guru* detaches himself or herself, because only through detachment can the experience become permanent. When we feel that the *Guru* is always available, we tend to take the shortcut and run outside, never fully believing in the guidance that we are getting from within. Therefore, for a while, the detachment has to be complete.

It is like the example I always give of being admitted in a hospital. When we are unwell, we need to go to the hospital for a while. Similarly, when we are attached, we need to detach for a while; and once we experience the Inner *Guru*, we will never be troubled by attachment! We will only be attached to our own Self, to the higher Consciousness. There will be no question of being attached to anyone and we will love everyone.

People ask how is it possible to love everyone without attachment? Actually, it is very simple to love selflessly. Since we are always connected with each other, we do what needs to be done without ever making the other person feel for it. There is no reason to tell anybody. A mother never tells the child how much she does for it. Similarly, a *Guru* never tells what he does for the persons he loves. It's just that the form becomes formless, which is the truth we have come to experience. Out of the highest compassion and love for his disciples, the *Guru* makes this act of sacrifice, because he knows that as long as his physical persona is accessible, the student will never get detached and will never experience the presence of the *Guru* within. Then, our love for our *Guru* goes up a hundred times over because we understand that, without his strictness and without his sacrifice, this experience would not have been possible. So, with much gratitude in our hearts for our *Guru*, who has significantly contributed to our present level of Consciousness, we will move on to today's subject, which is saying YES to life.

What do we mean by saying 'yes' to life? Now we have laid the ground and everyone has understood that life is just a game. We see it as a game because it has no stakes, for any stakes in this life are temporary and will soon be snatched away from us. None of our possessions, our relations and all that is so dear to us will remain and we won't be able to take them back home. Home is not the building we dwell in. It is where we are who we are, the eternal Consciousness. Whenever we are connected to our own Consciousness and experience a deep sense of peace and contentment where nothing else matters, we are at home. This feeling of being at home has nothing to do with the physical space. We keep saying that there is nothing like home because, when we travel somewhere out of town, we become restless and want to go back home. However, the day we start to feel at home everywhere, that is the day when we are completely connected to this one Consciousness.

When there are no stakes and no attachments, no heaviness from carrying unnecessary things, there is lightness. Those willing to let go and surrender must be already experiencing this lightness of spirit. Once that lightness comes, life becomes a great adventure and we start looking forward to it rather than dreading it. We start to look with great anticipation for what is going to happen next, because we are now ready for life. We understand it is a game in which we are becoming more skilful, and that there is nothing to get disturbed about. There's actually nothing to be done!

Whatever the situation and events the Consciousness, as a teacher, brings in front of us, we have to skilfully play the game well, like a good soccer, cricket or basketball player. We start to become very skilled at it because we are already feeling light and content. We are not playing for any result but because we must play, as there is no other choice. We are not running away scared and hiding in our homes, saying, 'Oh, my God, I don't want to go out, something may happen'. Rather, we are saying, 'Come life, let's play, you throw the ball and I am ready'.

We become ever ready, like a sprinter who is just waiting for the go. Instead of always reacting to life or hiding from it, we start watching with great enthusiasm what life is going to throw at us and show us. It is a great show that these senses perceive! We are being shown things, we are given experiences; and, by now, we have realised that every experience comes as a teacher so that we adapt, grow and evolve. There is no heaviness and this brings a sense of great joy. Let us always say yes to life. Whatever comes, let us be in full acceptance and ready for it.

What's got to happen will happen, whether we like it or not. The way we play and deal with it will change the course of all future events in our life. Do we wait in dread and pray that something does not happen or do we accept things and deal with them? We should be able to say, 'Come on! Bring it on, I am ready!'. It is a beautiful feeling because suddenly our outlook and attitude towards life has radically shifted. Nothing outside has shifted, neither our homes nor the clothes we wear nor the food we eat. Even whatever we have to do does not shift. The only thing that has shifted is something inside of us, because we are now in a completely different frame of beingness, of existence; not in a different frame of mind. We are looking forward to life and we are saying yes to life and to everything that is coming our way. The word 'no' just completely goes away. We say, 'Ok, if this is what has to be done, sure, I will do it. Let me see how I can do it'. The minute our Consciousness shifts to that, everything else starts to shift. We are no longer hiding from life. We are taking life head on. In turn, the Consciousness is immensely pleased with us because it has understood that we have learnt the greatest trick of life. We have learnt the greatest tool to successfully negotiate with what life throws at us. We have become that skilled player who knows exactly what needs to be done in a given situation. That is the confidence we get, which comes from our connection with the inner *Guru* or Consciousness.

We will never feel alone, scared or fearful in our heart, and there will be nothing in this world that we cannot do, because we will just feel light, present and wonderful while engaging with life. And this is the time when we re-engage back. Remember we had to detach for a while? It was a systematic withdrawal or isolation for a while, so we could experience the depth of our Consciousness, the truth of our being, the truth that we indeed are embodiments of love and light.

Something starts moving inside of us and, suddenly, that movement becomes almost like a dance because it gives us joy! What is the difference between walking and dancing? Walking is boring, dancing is joyous. The movement within becomes full of the joy we are seeking. I hope you are receiving this joy in your heart. It's not about the words, it's about what the energy is conveying to each one. That's the beauty. Some things are done by the body, some by words and some by energy. All three come together. A beautiful space which cannot be understood by the mind is created. It is the heart that is experiencing it. Something is happening that has not happened before. That something starts to shift everything for us. Therefore, the experience is essential because the process of shift has begun.

Thus, if we have shifted enough by now, we can say yes to life. We know that life will continue to create circumstances around us due to our past actions; and we cannot run away from them. But how we are going to approach life from this instant onwards can completely shift everything for us. Instead of being a receiver, we become a contributor. We contribute back to life and to people around us. This is because something has radically shifted and changed. That something cannot be defined or named, it can only be experienced in the heart.

CHAPTER 29: HAPPINESS IS YOUR NATURE

The previous chapter spoke about saying yes to life, no matter what came our way. We also said that once we understand that we are free and beyond attachments, we begin to look forward to life. We have enthusiasm inside of us and no longer have a defensive mindset. We take the bull by the horns, as we are ready for anything that comes our way. We are positive, we say YES, which means we accept all that is coming without fighting, denying or getting into self-pity. With this attitude and change of perception, everything starts to change for us. Things start to shift. We just need to hold on to faith for a while so that it helps us to take this experience. Actually, faith's job is only till we get the experience. Those who are living in the mind require faith. If we allow the mind to come in, it does not allow the Consciousness to do what it needs to. Once we transcend the mind and live only in the Consciousness, faith is no longer required because there is knowingness and beingness. So, we all have to go across and that can happen only by direct evidence (*Pratyaksha Pramana*), with our own experiences in life.

Once we open ourselves and go for the experience there is no going back, because then everything shifts for us. So, the struggle is only till that point. Before that, we have choices to make and our choices decide what happens to us. If you've seen the movie Matrix, they talk about taking a red pill or a blue pill. Which pill we take in life tells us what experiences we will have. We choose the pill of faith.

We keep saying that the mind cannot understand it fully. In fact it is not something to be understood, it is something to be experienced. When we accept what's coming our way and operate from the centre of our Consciousness, that Consciousness which is nothing but love incarnate starts to change everything for us. The mind is the heavy and dense part of us where the temporary sorrows and joys are kept.

Today, we are going to talk about happiness. Why is it that we only remember the unhappy experiences and put so much of our attention on our being unhappy. The answer is very simple. Unhappiness disturbs us because it is not our natural state. Our natural state is to be happy. So, whenever we are not in our natural state of being, we experience a sense of discomfort that we call unhappiness. We are always wanting to get back into our natural state. It is like a child, who is normally happy, giggling with joy and playing with whatever it can lay hands on, but starts crying the minute it becomes hungry or gets hurt. Crying is not the real nature of the child. The child cries to get attention from the parents, who will realise something is wrong and needs to be attended to.

It is the same with our unhappiness, which comes from the mind due to our desires, expectations, attachments and ego. Whenever that happens, we do not like it. We are unhappy because something inside of us is trying to pull us back. It tries to tell us that 'This is what I don't like'. That is the reason we are always seeking happiness, that is why our real nature is *Ananda* (bliss). So, what we are is what we are seeking. We are constantly yearning to be happy, but happiness cannot be bought. Otherwise, the richest people in the world should be the happiest ones. We know this is not necessarily true. When we look at poor people, especially in a country like India where there is so much poverty, the people are still happy. Actually if we look at poor people in general, the less they have the happier they are. Since they are ignorant about so many other things, just to get food two times a day gives them joy.

So, happiness is a state of mind. It is a state of being. It has nothing to do with our possessions or relations, as all these give only temporary joy. When we buy a new iPhone, our happiness lasts as long as the phone is new. The moment it falls and the screen is cracked, our happiness is gone. Our relations can be a source of joy as well as sorrow. If happiness comes from wealth and objects of desire, then rich people should be very happy. But even Alexander the Great wasn't happy after conquering half the world, because he realised that he had to leave this world empty handed.

Even though there is no connection of happiness with people and objects, all our life goes towards satisfying people and accumulating objects in our life. We are so outwardly consumed with all this, going through the cycles of joys and sorrows, that we never go in search of the permanent bliss which is within us, which is who we essentially are. And who we essentially are does not like to face those things that take it out of its inner state of being. Whenever there is unhappiness, it is actually a calling from Consciousness saying, 'I want to go home. This is not home. This is not who I am'. Slowly, our mind starts to understand that perhaps there is some other joy, something else which is a source of permanent happiness, which the five senses that are always running outwardly cannot experience. That joy is really the essence of what life is all about. To experience such joy and bliss, which is effortless and natural, no conditionalities are to be met. We do not require to be with certain people we like or to have certain things at all points of time. It does not depend on that. When we are really at home, which means being centred in our own Self, we experience the deep peace, happiness and oneness that we are seeking.

There is a story in the Upanishads of a King who was in search of happiness. He had great wealth, the strongest of armies, children and queens; yet, he was not happy. So, he called his ministers and asked them if they were happy at all times. They said they were not. Then, he asked them to find a person in the kingdom who was absolutely happy at all times. A wise man was called. The wise man said that, if they could find the shirt of a person who was happy all the time and the King wore it, then the King would become happy. So, they combed the entire kingdom looking for a person who was happy all the time! They all kept looking and asking everyone if they were happy all the time, but they could not find anybody.

In their search, they saw a cartman sitting under a cart straddled to a horse. He had taken shelter there since it was very hot, but he seemed to be in a state of absolute joy. The people approached him and asked him if he was a happy person, and the cartman said yes. They asked him if he was happy all the time, and he answered affirmatively. They asked him if he would give his shirt to the king but he didn't wear any shirt. So, they asked him to go and see the King, who was going to reward him. The cartman refused, saying that he did not need any reward. They told him that, if he did not go, he would be punished by the King, whereupon he said that he did not care since he was happy anyway.

The search party went back to the King and informed him they had found someone who was always happy, but who was not even responding to threats or promises of rewards. So, the King along with his ministers went to see this man. The King asked him what his secret of happiness was. If he were to share this, he would be given all the wealth that he needed. The cartman answered that he did not need anything and asked the King to go away. The King found it absurd that he had offered the man everything, but he was still not interested. Since he was quite determined to know the reason for that man's happiness, he went to see him again without taking any of his servants, as an ordinary person, and asked him to share the key of happiness.

The cartman said that, had the King come the first time without all his ego, he would have treated him well. Then, he told the King to sit and ask what he wanted. The King asked him why he was satisfied just being a cartman, and the man answered it just gave him a sense of joy all the time. The King offered to help him to get more resources so that, in addition to a cart he could also buy a boat to go fishing. 'What will I do with the fish?', asked the cartman. The King answered, 'You can sell it and get more money to buy more boats. 'What would I do with all that wealth?', asked the cartman. The King answered that it would make him happy. To that, the man answered, 'I am already happy. You must be a fool to try to offer all this to a person who is already happy and to whom all those things just don't matter'.

Now, if we were to reverse this story around, we would see that all our lives we are actually running after all things in order to become happy, but each time we get there we realise these things and these people are not giving us happiness. If we are always in search of happiness, it must be something very intrinsic and very basic. However, we never bothered to look inside of us to see if the source of happiness is lying there. It is that treasure we have always been looking for outside, but has always been inside of us. Happiness is our essential nature and that is why we have been searching for it. Happiness is who we are; joy is our state of being.

Everything that we have covered so far is interconnected and is now falling in place. As we go into this state of being aware of our Consciousness, all the worries, doubts and heaviness start to lift and suddenly we begin to feel peaceful and good about ourselves. It should be our endeavour to feel good all the time, not just sometimes. Permanent happiness is called bliss and that is the state we have set to experience for ourselves; that is, to experience the Godhood or the Universal Consciousness inside of us. When we are operating out of Consciousness, we experience peace, contentment and joy. Once we remain in that state, we have realised our true Self and we are operating from the Consciousness and not from the mind.

We know we have reached home when this state becomes permanent, when we are in a state of undisturbed peace. No matter what comes our way, no matter what challenges in life, we are ready to face them with enthusiasm, because there is joy in us and we are accepting life and saying yes to it. Magically, we start attracting everything in our life. That's the experience we have set ourselves for and that's the experience we are beginning to have.

CHAPTER 30: DO YOUR BEST LEAVE THE REST

Welcome to day thirty of the *Atma Chalisa Parayanam* (the journey of Self Realisation). We've spoken about saying yes to life and to all that life has to offer us. We said that we should be ready and enthusiastic, because happiness is our nature. It is what we've been seeking from the time we were born.

Who we are is what we attract in our life and, therefore, whenever we are unhappy we look for ways of trying to get out of it. The unhappy moments in our life remain with us and stand out for us because it is not in our nature to be unhappy. That is the reason why, when we are in our Consciousness, we feel a sense of deep peace, contentment and bliss, for this is who we are. Once we enter this zone where we are always connected with ourselves, we always feel at home; we always get that experience. The ultimate experience for us to know that we have reached the stage of Self-realisation is when we experience equanimity, *Sthitaprajna*, where nothing that happens outside affects us.

The nature of this *Samsara* (world) is to keep throwing challenges at us; but if we are joyously saying yes to life and looking forward to everything, then there is a solution for every challenge. We accept it and stop fighting. We just figure out how skilfully and perfectly we can do things. As we approach our life with this attitude, our perception towards everything changes. Slowly as we get more and more skilled at it, the reactions go away and we start becoming more and more perfect in whatever we do. And the place to practise this perfection is an imperfect world. If it were already perfect, how would we get to practise perfection?

The duality in this world gives birth to oneness. Since everything is dual, we must find this oneness in everything. By now, our understanding is clear. We have spoken about the law of opposing forces, where contradiction is part of this Creation. Day and night, good and bad are essential. Ultimately, we reach a point where we transcend good and bad, which are also a creation of the mind. That's why we say this whole Creation is nothing but an illusion. As long as we keep trying to intellectually understand, we will get lost since the mind cannot perceive that there can be contradictions, that there is good and there is bad.

The mind is a spiritual shopper. It does not want to do any hard work. It wants to analyse everything without even knowing how to experience it. So, we will shut the mind for a while but we will take it back at the right time and we will use this time to get the experience, the *Anubhava* (experience) or the *Pratyaksha Pramana* (direct evidence) or the *Swayam Anubhava* (self-experience). Once that starts to come, nobody needs to explain anything to us because it can't be explained. Nobody can take away our Self, our Consciousness, our state of joy.

Only *Sanathana Dharma* (The Eternal Way of Life practised by Indians) talks about experience. Every other religion forces us to accept things without experiencing them. Our saints and sages actually got things experientially first and then passed their findings unto us. There was no forcefulness on anyone. Faith was the only thing that the Masters asked from us, for we need faith in someone who has been on this journey and can be our guide. That person can get us the experience. Once this experience comes, it is undeniable, it cannot be taken away, it cannot be scammed or be artificial. We know that this is the real truth. We leave the stake of faith after we have directly experienced it. After getting the experience, we move beyond faith into the stage of knowingness. Ultimately, we will experience beingness, which is the last stage. In this state of being, all duality and all these laws we spoke about become inoperable. Though they are there, we go beyond them.

If we were to say Yes to life, then we must know how to perform our actions. This is the central essence of the Bhagavad Gita as well. It tells us,

> karmany-evadhikaras te ma phaleshu kadachana
> ma karma-phala-hetur bhur ma te sango
> 'stvakarmani
> (Bhagavad Gita Chapter 2, Verse 47)

Krishna tells Arjuna, 'Oh, Arjuna! Dedicate all your actions to Me, without any expectations, leaving the results to Me'. It simply means that, at all times, we should give our best and most honest effort, without expecting any results thereof. In other words, we do everything because we must do it, because that is what we feel compelled to do from within. We do things out of a sense of propriety, not seeking any gain, benefit or result. We do what we are being prompted to do from within, not getting swayed by the result or the impact it might have on others. We said that, when we do something in order to please others, we end up doing things that we did not intend to do. That is when we get caught in the knots of *Karma*. If we can learn the art of always doing everything from our sense of righteousness and perform actions without looking for any results, then such actions become non-binding and make the law of *Karma* inoperable. So, 'do your best and leave the rest'.

Therefore, the effects of such actions never hold us in the future. When we do such actions, we are actually surrendering them to the Universal Consciousness, whom we call God or Krishna. By saying we are surrendering them to the lotus feet of Krishna, we are saying we are surrendering them to Consciousness. We do the actions for the sake of doing them and not for any gain, benefit or impact. Once we get into the habit of performing actions like this, our inner sense takes over.

In every situation, we will instantly know what we need to do, without any doubts. On the other hand, when we do things from the mind, when we do them for someone, when we expect some result, when we do it for some particular gain, or we are trying to harm somebody, or if we are reacting from our mind, then we will always end up doing things which further and further bind us down in this game of life.

We have come here to learn how to free ourselves from the clutches of our *Karmic* account that we hold. The *Prarabdha Karma,* that *karma* which we have done in previous lifetimes, for which the scene has already been laid out for us in this lifetime, will have to be undergone by us. The future birth comes due to the mind because it still has attachments, desires, judgements, opinions etcetera. It is the mind that comes back as a new birth. So, once we start doing actions which are without expectation of result, then (a) the Karma is non-binding, and (b) when we go beyond the mind and always are focused on our consciousness, the mind becomes inoperable; and if we can live that life then there is no coming back because the mind is no longer there! Mind was never there! The mind always was and is an illusion.

The mind is a collection of thoughts and desires that we keep holding onto. The exercise of offering all the baggage we've been carrying to the *Trikuti* (*Guru Chakra*) is very powerful as it clears all our *Samskaras* (innate impressions). We must practise it intensely. Many times, we may think that thoughts are not coming and the *Trikuti* process need not be continued further, but actually we need to spend a lot of time with ourselves to be able to clear all this. As we sit in meditation, more and more things will keep coming because we are not only clearing this lifetime but also past lifetimes from our subconscious mind. It is akin to having a new birth since this extremely powerful technique clears out our subconscious mind.

The technique of how to act without getting bound by the results of our actions is to surrender them to the Consciousness.

We perform actions only because we must perform them; we must perform them from our sense of righteousness - D*harma*; and once we start doing it, we are then living our truth.

In the initial chapters, one of the first things explained was *Trikarana Shuddhi*- what we think is what we say and what we say is what we do. This is to be practised only for pure thoughts and not for negative thoughts. Once our thoughts have been purified, then we can definitely speak our mind and live our lives like that. In such a case, everything that had bound us so far would just start to go away from us. We start becoming much lighter since we operate at all times from our Consciousness. It is a very beautiful feeling. It is an experience which keeps coming to us as we walk fearlessly, because spirituality is nothing but fearlessness. Where does the fearlessness come from? When we have nothing to hide any longer, all fear disappears. We are fearful when we are hiding something or doing something wrong or when someone will say something to us. But, when our thoughts, words and actions are in alignment, when we are operating from the centre of our heart and we are offering all our actions based on righteousness to Consciousness, then there is no question of fear. That is how fearlessness will come; because we have become pure beings.

This understanding of how to perform actions is the basis of spirituality. This holds true for each and every action that we perform during the day. It could be cooking, cleaning, doing yoga, going out shopping, meeting people, working in the office or any other routine activity. If we start doing things without any expectations, either from ourselves or others, then slowly a shift happens in us. But, when we do something, we must give it our best shot, even though we have no expectation about the result. We just need to keep doing. However, if there is an error in what we are doing, then we must keep correcting it. We must keep doing, and what has to come to us will certainly come.

What goes wrong is the expectation; even for the result

there is an expectation. That is what is the attachment to the result. In a way, it is also an attachment. We are attached to the fact that we are doing something and we must get a result for it. That attachment is what we need to disconnect and move away from. We will automatically see results coming, because every action does have a reaction. But we are not expecting it or working for it. Then, our actions become a *Sadhana* (disciplined and dedicated spiritual practice), a penance, a *Parayanam* (intense practice). This is the best way to do *Chitta shuddhi* (cleansing the mind's sense of perception) as we start approaching everything from an authentic space, where we are able to align our thoughts, words and actions. This cannot happen unless we have surrendered to the higher Consciousness.

In our daily lives, a lot of times we get confused, we don't know what to do. Whenever there is confusion, we must always remind ourselves that we are thinking from the mind, which creates alternatives. But if we ask our heart, our Consciousness, we will know exactly what to do and we will never be misguided. Our mind may project adverse scenarios of how people may react to this, because they are not used to receiving things coming from the centre of that truth. But it is fine, it is their challenge. Soon, they will start respecting us because they will realise that only truth comes from our heart. The power of our words will leave an impact on them. Something in those words will get translated into energy, and that energy will make them change and shift.

So, it is an essential part of what we need to do, where do we come from and how do we start practising this. When we start examining every action of ours in this light, soon we will be able to find that balance and understand how it operates. We are trying to create an inner balance, do an inner tuning. Once that inner balance comes, we know exactly what it is about because the language of the Self is understood very clearly by the Self.

In the following chapters we will move into connecting all the dots of our lives and we will experience this whole understanding in totality.

CHAPTER 31: CUP OF HAPPINESS

Welcome to day thirty-first of the *Atma Chalisa Parayanam*. Yesterday, we spoke about how to perform our actions. When performing any action, big or small, we must give it our most honest effort, without expecting anything or trying to please anybody, and offering the result to the higher Consciousness. This action will stem out of righteousness or *Dharma*, since we would have purified our thoughts and they will be aligned to our words and actions.

Today, I will share something that came to me many years back, as a way of being happy at all times in our life. I was guided to come out with what I called the 'Cup of Happiness'. There is also a video of the same on YouTube. I don't know about other countries, but both in India and England we all love our cup of tea. So, inspired by the cup of tea, I said, 'Why not look at happiness as such?' Like we brew a cup of tea, we can actually brew happiness for ourselves.

Therefore, this cup is a metaphor for life and the tea that we are having is the tea of life. Each cup we take should make us feel happy, just like a cup of tea does. If we look at life simply, it consists of three things that are happening all the time. Either we are performing some action, or we are reacting to some action caused by others or we are engaged in an interaction. So, it is about action, re-action and inter-action. If we can remember how to act, how to react and how to interact, and what to avoid in these three circumstances, I think we should be pretty ok in life. We are doing this at the end of our entire series of overcoming the mind, operating from our Consciousness and knowing that our innate nature is happiness.

So, let's brew this beautiful tea of happiness. I am using a tea bag to represent what we are going to put in this cup. There are three tea bags that we use in life. One tea bag is to be used when we are doing an action, another one is to be used when we are reacting and the third tea bag is to be used when we are interacting.

Let's take the first tea bag of action. A tea bag has three parts to it. One is the bag which goes inside the cup; attached to the bag is a thread and the thread has a small paper flag from which we hold the tea bag. The flag is kept outside the cup and what goes inside is the bag part. The thread is basically just joining the bag and the flag. What is important for us in our lives is both the bag part and the flag part, which are interrelated. When we are acting, the bag part is called 'honest effort' or 'best effort' which we are going to give to life. Keeping our hand on our heart, we will say, 'This is my best effort. I have done what I could do in this situation'. It is easy because by now our mind has been purified our *Chitta* (sense of perception) has been purified and we are operating from our heart centre. So we can easily say that we have given it our best effort. That is all that is required - our best effort, our honest effort. The flag that we are keeping outside our cup is 'expectation of results'. We're not looking for recognition or rewards, and we are not trying to please anybody. We are performing that action because it is being prompted to us from within. Such actions are called *Dharmic* actions. They come from our sense of righteousness. So that is what we do when we drink the tea of action.

The second tea bag is that of reaction. Many times, we react to situations that come to us. In this tea bag of reaction, the bag part is called 'forgiveness' and the flag part is called 'negativity'. Whenever somebody says to us something we don't like, something unfavourable or untrue, instead of getting into an argument or creating negativity about the person which makes us react, we quickly do a prayer of forgiveness in our heart. That prayer was given to us by Jesus Christ when He said, 'Forgive them for they don't know what they are doing'.

Forgiveness is a beautiful energetic cleanser. Every time we don't instantly clear with forgiveness whatever has hurt us, it gets deposited in our subconscious mind as *Samskaras* (innate impressions), which create problems for us energetically even though we don't think so consciously. Forgiveness is like a balm, like a cleanser. We have already talked about how we can use the *Trikuti* or *Guru Chakra* meditation to clear whatever gets energetically stored as *Samskaras* in our mind. We tend to carry *Samskaras* of negative experiences like hurt, pain etcetera, and forget the good things. Somebody cheated on us and we keep holding onto it, thus creating a challenge for ourselves. One negativity leads to another and another, and we become a powerhouse that attracts negativity all the time. So, when we are reacting, we must keep the bag of forgiveness inside the cup and keep the flag of negativity outside.

Now, let's come to the third tea bag. It is called the tea bag of interaction. We are always interacting with people who live or work with us or who we meet regularly. How should we interact with them? In this third tea bag, the bag part we keep inside our cup is 'love' and the flag part we keep out is 'judgement'. When we judge others, we can never love them and when we love them, we can never judge them.

So in our interaction with people, especially our families, our friends and all those who are actually constantly interacting with us, with them we need to use the tea bag of interaction which means all interactions coming from our heart will flow through with love and we will keep the judgement out. Never judge your loved ones, never say, 'Oh he or she is like that...' The minute we do that, we have already created a negative doorway. We have created a distance between us and our loved one. Especially in the closest relationships this is a major cause of our problems because what we do is that we label them. For example, we say that this person is from the mind and I am from the heart or we say that that person is always doing this and I am doing that, therefore I have to always react. This is incorrect and exactly where the challenge lies. So we must go into the space of love and say that this person is exactly who he or she is, and exactly the same Consciousness which is in me which makes me divine is also coursing through the person in front of me.

Every interaction, every person and every situation in our life is nothing but a teacher; and there are going to be tough teachers, since we don't learn from loving teachers as much as we learn from tough teachers. We have stubborn minds and sometimes we are not open to learn certain lessons which keep coming to us lifetime after lifetime. Therefore, we need somebody really strong to come and hammer it on us. It is like someone persistently knocking on our door and saying, 'Hey, wake up!' That's our challenge. Especially close relationships we can't get rid of come as teachers for us, but we acknowledge that. We keep thinking how bad the situation is for us and start fighting against it. In the process we create walls in trying to deal with it. So please use the bag of love for in love there is no judgement. If we have judged, love just does not come and that spoils the relationship. But love just opens everything and creates miracles in our lives. People may not show it to us, but love never ever goes waste.

Whenever we are either reacting or interacting, it should be from our heart centre, which means that we are coming out of love; we're sharing love with others so it keeps the negativity out. When somebody says something to us negatively, something that hurts us, then first of all we must forgive that person; forgiveness not for the namesake, but from the heart. We should hold our hand on our heart and then say 'I forgive you, I forgive you, I forgive you'. Then tell that person, 'I love you, I love you', and cover the person with the white light of love. Surround the person energetically and that starts to shift everything for us. We must energetically make sure that clearance is happening otherwise the negativity will cling onto us. Mere words by themselves won't do anything.

Also, in this cup of life, we need a sweetener. It is called 'acceptance'. If we are in complete acceptance of people and situations, it will help us to enjoy our actions, our reactions and our interactions. We will not be creating conditionalities around things, but we will have unconditional acceptance. In this play of life, all the actors are coming around us only to give us something. If we accept them as teachers, we can love them; but when we put them in the buckets of negative and positive, we get caught up in those emotional bundles, the mind takes hold of us and the *karmic* accounts grow. So, the sweetener that we are using is called unconditional acceptance. And when we put a sweetener to our cup, we also need a stirrer. It is called awareness. We should stir the cup of life with the awareness of who we truly are. We are not the body nor the mind. We are Consciousness. We are that which is seated in our heart through which love flows. We are that which is present everywhere. We are that creative life force. That is the truth of our being.

If we look at every action, reaction and interaction through the lens of acceptance and awareness, bringing the awareness of who we truly are, suddenly everything changes. However, when we see ourselves as individuals with a limited consciousness, the mind comes in and we start seeing things differently. The minute we put the awareness of divine Consciousness everything shifts. As we get into practising the presence of this Consciousness inside of us, the witness starts to grow and we are able to see things very differently from how we have seen them so far. Then, problems don't remain as problems. Challenges become something to learn and grow, and we become enthusiastic as we see it all as a game. Soon, we become skilled exponents of this craft called life, we exude love and this love flows to everyone. That is what we're beginning to experience.

The cup of happiness has all the essential ingredients that

we need on a daily basis. So, if we have this cup two times a day, morning and night, then happiness is guaranteed.

Note: Please refer to the Appendix section for a chart with the recipe to follow for The Cup Of Happiness

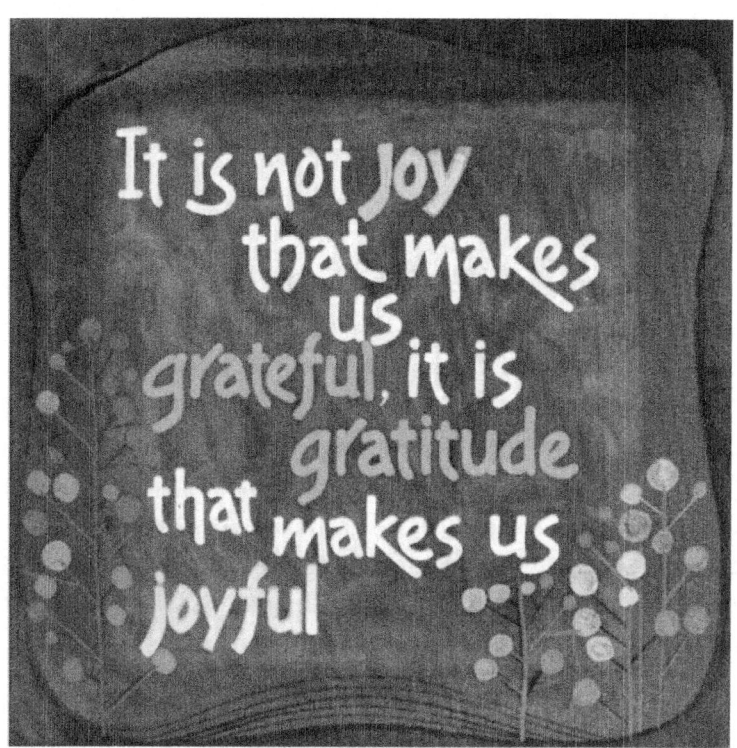

CHAPTER 32: GRATITUDE ALWAYS

Welcome to day 32 of the *Atma Chalisa Parayanam*. We are now going into the last state of 'beingness'. We've done the whole journey from belief to faith and from faith to experience that gave us knowingness. From knowingness, we shall go into beingness. A very powerful and most beautiful thing that brings abundance and joy into our lives is gratitude. It is so magical and simple, and we are all aware of it, but we have never focused on it and that is the reason for all our problems. We live in a world where everyone and everything is connected to each other at all times. Our existence is not in isolation but in co-existence.

As we know, every thought prompts an action and every action has a reaction. It has a reflection and a resound that comes back to us. So, a mere thought sets up a chain of events and triggers a series of actions, reactions and interactions. Now, when we combine the thoughts of seven billion people living on this planet, we simultaneously create both - beauty and harmony on one hand and chaos and conflict on the other. That is the reason why this game of life is played till perpetuity. We often ignore the beauty and harmony, but we focus on chaos and conflict because our mind always goes towards what is wrong, what is negative or what is missing as we are able to spot that easily. As our mind gravitates towards negativity, the resultant thoughts further exacerbate the chaos and conflict on our planet.

We know that this is all a game and that the game can end only when everyone becomes thoughtless. Just imagine a world where we're devoid of thoughts! I don't think it's going to happen anytime soon. So, why don't we change our focus?

Why don't we start appreciating beauty and harmony in the world, instead of looking at negativity? Imagine what kind of thoughts we could create! We would create thoughts of beauty, joy and happiness, and negativity would be completely replaced by something beautiful. We would transform this planet into a place of truth, auspiciousness and beauty, *Satyam, Shivam, Sundaram.* So, why don't we change our thoughts and start appreciating everything around us instead of focusing on what is missing?

We can start expressing our gratitude for the air we breathe, the food we eat, the ground on which we stand, the place where we sit, the house where we live in, the jobs that we have, the businesses that we do, the clothes that we have, the books that we read. We can start showing gratitude to plants, animals, insects, flowers, trees, clouds, sky and water. We can be grateful to all the people who are doing so much for us, like the farmer, the baker, the cook, the doctor, the *Guru*, the builder, the tailor and even our governments. We can feel gratitude towards our nation, the people, our *Satsanga*, our parents, our friends and God. If our lives can become full of gratitude for all that we have, we shall always experience abundance, harmony and joy.

So, why wait to become thoughtless? Why not change our thoughts into thoughts full of gratitude? Isn't that a very beautiful way to start transforming the whole world? What is gratitude? 'I thank you' When I say 'Thank you' to you, you also say 'Thank you' to me. In other words, when I give gratitude to you, you give gratitude back to me, so a positive energy goes from me to you as well as from you to me. Since the entire creation is a play of energy, when these positive energies are exchanged, they will always bring good and happy tidings in our life, as the Vedas say, *Shubham, Shubham, Shubham* – all that is auspicious, auspicious, auspicious. It will come in our lives because of gratitude; that's the power of gratitude.

Every morning and night, we should pray and express our

gratitude to all those who bring us all that we need. We should do a prayer and thank all the people around us, all that we have and Nature. It will always bring abundance in our lives. Though I occupy a small room and live minimalistically, yet I experience extreme abundance. Everything just comes to me. A thought may occur to me and it gets fulfilled! All due to this power of gratitude. I am sure everyone has experienced the power of gratitude at some point in our lives. It's just that now we are focusing on it to bring it into our conscious awareness.

So, I hope we all will consciously add gratitude to our daily cup of happiness and experience the magic of abundance and auspiciousness unfold!

CHAPTER 33: CHOICELESS AWARENESS

We have already embarked on the last section of our journey, which pertains to remaining in a state of beingness. So, we've crossed from knowingness into beingness. If we can stay in a state of gratitude at all times, it attracts all the positive energies to us and our focus goes away from the negative things that are happening around us. The minute we shift our consciousness into the energies of gratitude, it starts to bring abundance in our life, and that's a very magical way of living. We have already learnt how to perform our actions, how to react and how to interact. This is the knowingness part of it. But, then, how do we BE? How do we remain? What's the state of being in our day-to-day living?

Gratitude is a very valuable part of this journey. It is a great start; a wonderful way of living life. It is beautiful to be able to say thank you and pay gratitude to everyone, whether it is our children, our husband or wife, our neighbours, all the elements of nature, environment, etcetera. If we can see what an important and valuable contribution they are making in our journey, it just fills our heart with gratitude. And that gratitude spreads like magic. The energetic balance in us starts to shift and we remain in that state of centredness.

Today, we will take the second step forward in the state of beingness, which is to be in choiceless awareness. What is choiceless awareness? It simply means to be always aware of the truth of our being, which is beyond the mind, which is Consciousness. Awareness is the focus of our attention. If we stop paying attention to our mind, if we do not comply with its urges and tendencies and if we just learn to observe the thoughts that are coming and going, then we start to remain in the awareness of Consciousness. We become aware of the Presence within us.

When we are in choiceless awareness, we have no particular choice of being in a certain state. We are not choosing proactively to be either this or that. We are not seeking anything from our side. We are neither wanting to be happy nor wanting to keep sadness away. We are not wanting to be in a particular place or do a particular thing. We are in a state of neutrality, which means that we are open at all times to all that Consciousness brings to us. We are ever ready and we are looking at things with a sense of adventure, with joy in our heart, because we've understood that life is nothing but a game. By now, we have become very skilled at this game because, in the last thirty-three days, we have left behind all the heaviness that our mind had been carrying on this beautiful journey.

We are now able to face the so-called surprises of life and tackle them without losing our enthusiasm. We are able to solve even the knottiest problems, because we are seeing everything as a beautiful game of Consciousness. Since we've now started to operate from there, we are able to see a daily improvement in our ability to watch our thoughts as we deal with life. Things start to shift and, all of a sudden, the steering wheel of our life is back in our control. We are no longer thrown away by the vagaries of life, by situations that used to put us out of balance. We have now reached this point because we have done enough *Manana* (contemplation) and we have started to practise.

The sages before us have called it a state of choiceless awareness. We have no choice because the ability to make a choice comes from the mind, and we are operating out of Consciousness. We are able to do this because we know that Consciousness is super intelligent and super intuitive. It has a plan, it has a way of doing things and it is always in control. Therefore, we rest in *Ananda* (bliss). We are aware of the truth that this game of life is not going out of control, so there is no anxiety left. We're not thinking, 'Oh my God, what's going to happen if I miss this?' We know that situations will always work out somehow so that we are able to do what we are yearning to do, and that makes us start feeling more settled and balanced. It doesn't matter any longer what is going to come our way; we are always ready and we are not particular about things happening in a certain manner. It makes us spontaneous and free, because we know that all is coming from Consciousness and not from the mind that creates roadblocks and challenges.

How can we remain in the state of Consciousness or beingness? It is such a beautiful feeling to live a life away from the clutches of the mind, the screaming that goes on in our head and the compulsions that we've had to deal with. Suddenly, we come to this beautiful ocean of peace where we are ever content and yet we are not lazy. Contentment and choicelessness does not mean that we are just going to sit in *Padmasana* (yogic posture) doing meditation. Of course not! Instead, we are ready for all that Consciousness prompts us to do, because by now we've stilled our mind and we've been able to recognise when something is coming from Consciousness. When we start operating, all our actions and experiences out of those actions tell us that it is coming from Consciousness, from the heart, and not from the mind.

That stillness, that silence, that peace, the removal of reactions and the sense of anticipation and joy is the experience of *Ananda,* that comes when we are in the awareness of Consciousness, that comes from the right understanding that we are not the body-mind duo, but the immortal being that resides in this complex of body and mind. It is that permanence which does not get destroyed because of the changing body and mind.

So, we started off our journey thirty-three days back with acquiring the right knowledge. We removed the darkness of ignorance from our mind, we got our facts right, we understood the laws that operate around us and then we started to move into an experiential journey. Now, we're coming to that point when we're beginning to identify what it means to be in the state of awareness so that this experience is just not a blip but something that remains with us. It is that presence which we are experiencing at this point in time; and the game of life is all about experiencing this presence and being in this presence (*Sat Chit Ananda*). Once the truth dawns on us, and all the clouds of misunderstanding are removed and the *Chitta* begins to shine, the awareness starts to come. The resultant experience, the state of being, is of bliss.

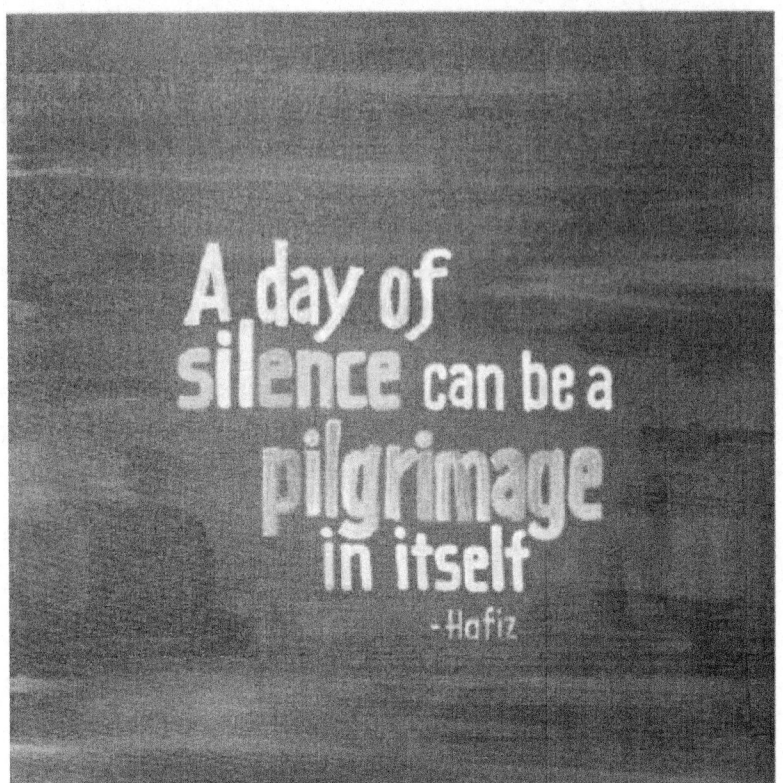

CHAPTER 34: SILENCE AND STILLNESS

Welcome to day 34 of the *Atma Chalisa Parayanam.* Yesterday we discussed a state of being where we are operating from neutrality, from choiceless awareness, where we are fully aware, alert and attentive to Consciousness. We have no particular preferences or ideas. We are in a zone of neutrality where we are just being. At the same time, because we are connected to Consciousness or the Supreme Intelligence, we feel that we are ready, prepared and equipped to deal with all the so-called challenges and situations that come into our lives. We are neither running away from anything nor we are running towards anything. We are in a state of readiness which comes from our connection, familiarity and oneness with Consciousness. That, along with the power of gratitude which becomes a way of life for us, starts attracting all that is good or, as the Vedas say, all that is *Subham-* the auspicious. All that is good and auspicious starts to make a beeline towards us, as if there is some nectar inside of us and all the honey bees want to come towards us. We start attracting Nature, because actually we're part and parcel of Nature. This connectedness takes us to the point of stillness.

So, today, we are going deeper and deeper inside our own Self, which is expansive and vast. It is a space of stillness, in which we experience Consciousness. It is not the stillness that comes from lack of movement. It is that stillness which is inherent in motion, because Consciousness is always freely flowing. Consciousness is in an inherent state of movement and it is moving all around. Consciousness in movement is expressed as *Jagat,* what we see around us. However, the innate essence of Consciousness is stillness. Again, the contradiction comes - there is stillness in the flow, there is stillness in movement. We do not experience this stillness by becoming motionless or sitting in meditation. We experience it when we get connected to the source, to Consciousness. We feel still inside, while everything around us is going on.

This stillness is born out of the receptacle of silence. It is not due to the absence of noise. It is a silence which is there despite all the noise around us because this is the very nature of Consciousness. Consciousness is still and silent. It is a beautiful space that lies beyond the mind, a space of absolute calmness and stillness. It feels almost like a void or a vacuum which produces this silence. It's not a physical silence but an inner experience. So, feel this inner silence- so peaceful and still. This silence is so expansive that, as we keep going within, it just keeps sucking us inside and, the deeper we go, the more we get enveloped by this stillness.

This is a place where the true Self reveals itself in its full radiance and brilliance; as if the pearl of the Self, the shining light of the Self reveals itself to us in the darkness of this void, this vacuum. It is like the most brilliant and shining star that is there all around us, and we become aware of Consciousness, that is untainted, pristine, pure and absolutely harmonious. It is blending in this darkness and yet it is full of light. It is the stark darkness of the void which creates the beauty and majesty of this brilliant radiance of the Self. Again, the contradiction plays itself. We realise that that is how it is; that is how the play is - light comes out of darkness and the connection with the Self gets established. All the restlessness in the body and the mind ends and we feel content, complete, whole and absolutely fulfilled. We experience an energetic Presence that is all knowing and skilful.

At first, the connection is intermittent. We see it, we don't see it, we see it... Slowly, over a period of time, this experience becomes constant and we become comfortable with this Consciousness. As our awareness grows, we keep going deeper into the depths of this ocean of silence, we start getting connected to this unknown source of wisdom that always seems to know everything. The intuitive knowingness is the connection of our inner consciousness with the all-pervading Universal Consciousness. The void or the darkness is actually the womb from which the Universal Consciousness is born which gives us all the wisdom, all the knowledge and all the understanding. From this dark void, brightly sports forward this individual consciousness to which the void feeds all the knowledge and understanding. We feel comfortable with this duality, with the presence of this darkness. No longer does it bring fear, since we understand that everything is born out of this duality. This Universal Consciousness is the centre of everything and it is a part of who we truly are.

Therefore, we understand that all the play that happens outside of us is the play of the Consciousness within. The duality outside of us is part of that same oneness; it is just a play, a projection, a manifestation. We understand that the entire control is within, not outside. As we start to remain in this stillness and this connectedness, our world outside starts to magically change. The play between the individual consciousness or *Jeevatma* and the Divine Consciousness or *Paramatma*, starts to merge. The boundaries between dark and light start to blur and everything becomes that one light. When this mergence takes place, everything becomes that one light. The feeling is like that of a child who finally comes home to the mother's love, the mother's wisdom and, most importantly, the mother's protection. We know we are safe, since the Mother is going to take care of us. To experience this oneness is the quintessential search of all of us. To remain in the light of this awareness while we perform the *Dharma* of this body is actually the essence of Self-realisation - the goal of our life. To perform all actions in the noise and din of this world, with the inner stillness born out of detachment is the attribute of a *Jeevan*

Mukta or a liberated being.

Such a person is not bound by the consequences of her or his actions. For such a person, the head is in the forest and the hands are in society. Head in the forest means absolute stillness, as if meditating in the silence of a dense forest, not distracted by the vagaries of the mind. Hands in society means willingness to perform service to all those who are in need. We have all been born with some gift that has been given to us. That's the gift we've come to share with everyone, because everyone is a reflection of our own Self. Once we are comfortable with this stillness, when we are connected to the source, when we are comfortable with this darkness, when we are comfortable operating in the silence amidst all the noise, then we are eternally at home. We are liberated from the mind, which keeps bringing us back, and this cycle of birth and death completely comes to an end.

So, for each one of us, this die has been cast. The mould has been set. We have all dived deeper and deeper with every passing day, and now the pieces of ourselves have come together into this state of beingness, into this state of Consciousness, into this state of understanding our experiences. We know that we are in a zone of absolute safety because we have come in connection with the Lord Almighty, the God Supreme, the Consciousness to whom we have been praying all the time, whose guidance we have been seeking, for whom we have been willing to do all that it takes. That One to whom we have prayed has now majestically revealed itself as none other than the Self, as none other than our own Consciousness.

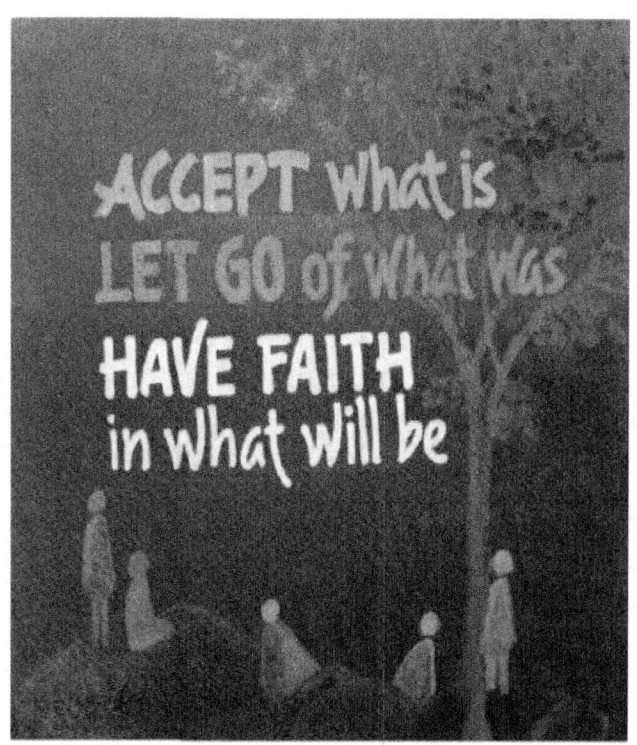

CHAPTER 35: LET GO AND FLOW

Welcome to day thirty-five of the *Atma Chalisa Parayanam*. *Hanuman Jayanti* (birthday of Sri Hanuman ji) is being commemorated today in Karnataka; so, we wish a happy birthday to Hanuman ji! Hanuman ji's birthday is celebrated many times during the year. In the north, it is celebrated in the month of April, that is, on the full moon of the month of Lord Rama's birthday. Here, they are celebrating it today, so it's relevant that we talk about him because of today's topic.

Silence and stillness are always with us, even when we are in motion or in a crowd; but they leave us when we are troubled by our mind, thoughts, attachments and expectations. So, in one minute we are in absolute stillness and calmness, thinking we've moved far ahead, and suddenly we fall prey to our expectations! We expect things from our loved ones and the people around us, and when these expectations are not met, that gives rise to anger. Suddenly, we lose that stillness and silence inside of us. The root cause of all these fluctuating emotions is our attachment.

As long as attachments are there, as long as we cling on to the people who we think are ours, we will continue to face this. There is a blog I wrote in November, 2017. It was a cry from a heart which did not want to participate any longer in this world of attachments, of expectations and disappointments. At the same time, it was also a yearning to be absolved from this *Maya* (illusionary world), from the clutches of this maddening delusion caused by our attachments, which are round the corner, always ready to spoil our peace and get us out of our Consciousness. Today, five years after that cry to the Mother, I feel that if the yearning is intense, if the desire is pure and if we are ready to walk that path, then the love which we have come to experience and share with everyone starts to gush forth and flow. Each one of us can be that Apostle of Love.

What is it to let go and flow? How is it a contributor in our journey? The state of beingness is actually equivalent to what we call as let go and flow. We have spoken many times about letting go. What does it mean to let go and what are we trying to let go of? It could be that things are not going as per our plans. Mind likes to plan, but Consciousness may have other plans and things may not go as per the plans of our mind. So, if we accept the will of Consciousness instead of getting upset, in that moment we let go. If people are being inconsiderate and unreasonable to us, we don't bear grudges with them, we don't judge them, we let go and forgive them, for they are operating out of ignorance and we are suffering because of our attachments, so we must let go!

We take actions out of fear of making mistakes, instead of letting the divine love in our heart guide us. Let's not get hung-up on these transitory actions, since they are part of the illusion and don't mean anything. Let us observe and not react, let go and be patient! Eventually, the love in our heart will prevail, because that is the language of Consciousness, which is supremely intelligent.

Sometimes we find that actions are discriminatory against us, rather than being discriminated or discerned upon. Let's not be uptight about the whole idea of right and wrong, because it comes from the mind. Let go; Truth shall prevail. It always prevails in the end. We do not have to prove a point. We do not have to go and wallow in self-pity. Many times, especially when people are walking together on the path of spirituality, we find that separations are created. We should not fret, since it's an old human failing. Just let go, knowing that the river ultimately finds its way to the sea and all these are just testing points.

So, my fellow journey men and women, the panacea for

all that you are presently experiencing, have experienced in the past and will experience in the future, is the *Maha Mantra* (highest *Mantra*) 'Let Go'! Do not hold onto any preconceived idea. No thought. No belief. No opinion. No judgement. Let go of all the past conditioning! Put everything in the fire of *Trikuti* (*Guru Chakra*). Simply let go! The present time is all about letting go and flow. What do we mean by flow? What is the sensation of flowing? Flow simply means to just BE without any conditionalities, prejudices or preconceived ideas. To flow means to be in a blank state and not resist what is happening.

I will give an example. We know that a river is in a constant state of flow, right from its origin on the top of the mountains, where the snow starts to melt. It continues to flow down into the valleys and plains, until it merges into the sea. I experienced it first hand when I went river rafting and had to wear a life jacket. I simply jumped into the river Ganges and, for almost one kilometre, I flowed freely downstream. It was such a fantastic feeling! Just imagine! You are lying in the lap of Mother Ganges and, without any effort, you are being simply taken ahead. The river is so mighty that, even if you were to make an effort, it would be futile. So, instead of trying to fight the current, you just simply float and go with it. The river is taking you where you need to be taken and you're wearing protective gear.

What is this protective gear? In the manner a life jacket protects a person floating in the river, our Consciousness is our life jacket protecting us from all harm or danger in life, because the divine aspect of the Self is in control. The only thing out of control is our mind. It is the mind which makes us go against the flow, swim against the flow of Consciousness. Everything is happening as per the perfect plan of Consciousness, of which we are a part. It's just that we have been swimming upstream, rather than downstream. We have been resisting because of our ideas, attachments and feelings due to which we keep coming back again and again. It's a whirlpool in which we find ourselves stuck.

If we let go, if we float and go with the tide, without the encumbrances of the mind, without applying brakes all the time, I can tell you it's an incredible feeling. Buddha called it the 'void'. The Vedas call it *Shunya*. Taoism calls it the *Tao*. I simply call it flow. Just let go and flow. As we start flowing, we find our centre, we find our Self. In the flow, there is a void. In the movement, there is *Shunya*. It is that *Tao*, that Consciousness which is making everything happen. Why is it so difficult to let go? Why is it so difficult to simply flow through life? Look at children, they don't even have to let go; they are always just flowing because their mind has not got activated yet. Look how Nature flows! The wind is blowing, the water is flowing, the fire is moving, the Earth is rotating and everything flows in this illusion of space.

Hanuman is such a beautiful example of flow. He never thought it was impossible to go and catch hold of the sun! At that time, his mind was not working; he was young and he simply went. Any grown up with a mind already in place would have said that it was not possible. But, since he wished to reach the big bright ball in the sky, he went with the flow and put the sun in his mouth. When he had to go and look for Mother Sita, while the other monkeys said they wouldn't be able to jump over the sea, he just believed in what his Master had said. He did not use his mind. He just said that, if his Master believed he could do it, and if he had faith in him, then of course he could do it. This is an example of letting go. When he had to get the *Sanjeevani Buti* (life providing herb that grew in the Himalayas) for Lakshmana within twenty-four hours, he just went with the flow and brought the entire mountain back.

When we flow, we do not avoid things and run away from them. Yes! We avoid confrontations, we avoid unhappiness, because we are using the bag of forgiveness, of love, of our best action, with the awareness of our Truth and the sweetness of acceptance. Once acceptance comes in, we are able to let go. Once we let go, we flow with that one Consciousness. If we can be in acceptance of this universal rhythm which is perfect in nature, then we are also born to be perfect, whole and complete because we are born out of Nature; are an aspect of Nature. So, how can any external imperfections of people, places, situations or circumstances drag us down from our natural state?

Every time we get stuck in a situation, let us remember who we are and simply let go and flow with the river. Let's put that image in our head: flow with Hanuman, fly in the sky, go with the flow. Do not go against the flow. When we go against the flow, it means the mind is there. The heaviness will come and we will instantly know we are going against the flow. The mind says, 'I have to be somewhere; I have to do this!' Then, we are going against the flow. When we are in the flow, everything happens as the higher Consciousness wants. All circumstances change when we come in the flow. We learn to float in the same direction as the Consciousness and this extremely intelligent super Consciousness takes us.

The other thing that happens when we are in the flow is that we are always in the present moment. We are acutely and perfectly aware of the present moment. That is the state of beingness which we have been describing in the last few days. Choiceless awareness, attitude! This is our natural state, where everything starts happening spontaneously because there's no longer a dragging effect. It is not a question of trying and things not happening. Trying will come when we have not understood. Trying means we do not want to do it. When we have understood it fully then things happen in an instant.

There's no question of attachments dragging us down as long as we have decided to do something about it. However, if we have not made up our mind to do something about it, then of course it is a pretty difficult task, a very heavy effort because we are trying to convince our mind but it is not getting convinced and we are just not willing to let go. When we let go, we don't lose anything! It's just our mind which has created insecurities and fears, telling us something is going to happen. Nothing happens except for the joy that comes in our life, except for the total peace that we experience! We don't have to rely on anyone else other than our own Consciousness.

So, this was the next state of beingness, of operating from our Consciousness, from the truth of our being, which is ever present, which is all knowing and which is the Creator Himself and, therefore, is omnipotent. When we are in that space, all heaviness just goes. As we pray to the Mother to grant us her grace, we must let go of this girlfriend called mind, which is carrying all these attachments; and the Mother's blessings will come, because they were never away from us.

Shraddhavan labhate jnanam

The one who seeks with intense devotion knowledge of the Self

Yad bhavam tad bhavati

What you intensely feel and yearn for manifests in your life

CHAPTER 36: LOVE INVERTER

As we steadily progress in this journey of beingness, we shall discuss the essence of this beingness and the essence of this Creation. We are coming to the ultimate destination, which is both the source, the journey and the destination. It is the cause, the effect and the continuance. I'm talking about the primal energy, the primal essence of all existence, of all of beingness, which is love.

Let us visualise the river Ganges. Right from the top of the mountain, it is in a constant state of flow. As it flows, it carries with it all who wish to accompany it on the journey, be it boulders, pebbles, stones, mud, fish, branches, trees and even human ashes or bones. Not for a minute does the river say, 'Hey! I'm not going to carry you, O' boulder. I'm not going to carry you, O' fish! I'm going to just travel by myself. You have not paid me anything, so why should I hold your load or carry you?' The river just doesn't do that. As it flows, it carries everybody and everything along. It does not hold any prejudice. It takes the swimmers, the surfers, the boats and the canoes. And, as the journey of each one comes to an end, the river continues to flow. It does not get attached to any of the objects that have travelled with it. It does not say, 'You come along and continue to travel with me'. It leaves everything where it belongs or where it needs to go. It does not ask for a reward, a return or a favour. It does not discriminate whether the bush is poisonous or is providing fruit. It does not discriminate whether the boulder is big or small. Regardless, it carries everything along with it.

This is the lesson we learn from every element of Nature, be it the Sun that keeps shining or the wind that keeps blowing. They do not wait and stop to say, 'I will not shine on the home of a sinner, I will shine only on the home of the one who has a good heart'. The air and the wind do not differentiate between a sinner and a saint, between the good, the bad and the ugly. They do what needs to be done, without getting attached to any particular aspect of Nature. They do what they have to do because they must, because that is their true nature. We all need to imbibe the very nature, the very essence, that makes us do what we must do, which is to love unconditionally.

The difference between human love and the love expressed by the river, the Sun and the wind is that human love, though it starts very purely, doesn't remain so. When a child is born and comes into this world, its fist is clenched. Why is it clenched? Because it carries with it a gift from the other world. And who's the first recipient, who's the first one who opens its hands and gets this gift? It is the mother. The child bears the gift of love and gives it to the mother. This woman, who was just like any other person till that moment, as soon as she receives that gift of love from the pure one, suddenly starts feeling so much of love for the child, because it has received the gift of pure love. There are changes which a woman undergoes the minute she becomes a mother. As the child grows and plays, and the mother enjoys this love and showers it back on to the child, she slowly starts to become attached to it and her love starts to get constricted. It becomes full of fear and selfishness. Slowly this love that the child brings to share with the world soon starts changing from divine love into human love, which is full of attachments and expectations; and the pure flow of love starts to get constricted with conditionalities and experiences.

His entire life, man is in search of that pure love; but he always has conditionalities put to it. He is always seeking something in return for the love he gives and shares. He is not able to love selflessly although, like the river, his nature as a human being is to love. This gift of love which he came with is pure and has no attachments or expectations; it is love for the sake of love, love that comes from a pure heart. When the time comes for us to leave this world, the clenched fist opens and we go empty handed. We go back to God and He says, 'When you left, I gave you a gift. Where is the gift that I gave you?' The man shows his calloused, bruised and wrinkled hands and says, 'God, my hands are empty. I lost the gift'. Then, God says, 'Ok, go back again till you learn to keep the gift with you and share it with all. I gave you this gift to expand and grow it and not to hold it only for yourself'.

So, we are talking about that love which is based on selflessness, on sharing and caring, regardless to whom we are sharing it with. Sometimes, we find it easy to love those who we do not know, but very difficult to love our neighbours or the people about whom we know everything. That is because we judge them; and when we judge, love disappears. That's why Jesus said, 'Love thy neighbour first'. If we can love our neighbour, if we can love the one whose negative traits we know, then we can truly learn to love.

This love is brimming inside each one of us. As we go beyond the mind, as we start experiencing gratitude in our life and as we start living a life of choiceless awareness, when stillness comes to us and we start experiencing this flow, we suddenly realise we've reclaimed the gift back. It was always there, inside each one of us. It was just covered under layers and layers of expectations and attachments, judgements and opinions that this limited human experience has brought to us. Then, this love starts to gush forth once again. If we restrict or control anything which is meant to flow, it does not like it. The minute it is set free, it just knows how to flow. When the matrices and hard edifices we had got stuck in suddenly begin to dissolve, we start getting our precious gift back. Everything starts to magically happen in our life and we experience joy like never before.

This love starts to come out from every cell of our body, from every pore of our skin, from every hair, and we experience its warmth. This love is expansion! We never fall in love. It is the human love in which we fall. In divine love, we rise, we expand and we embrace others. It's not physical love; it's a love which knows no boundaries. It is the love which we are experiencing in this moment, as it flows to each one of us from the source of Consciousness and is received by our love which is also from the same source. All differences merge and, suddenly, magic starts to happen. Something beautiful inside of us starts expressing itself. Love cannot be explained in words. Love can only be experienced. There is a lightness, calmness, beauty and sweetness in this love. There is a feeling of bliss, because this love is not just for the people around us, but is available to everyone at all times. It sees no separation, it sees no boundaries, it does not distinguish between 'mine' and 'thine'.

Let this love pour out of us! This the love of the Golden Age, the age of love. This is the very essence of the Self. Let us experience the joy of love in us. Let us experience the energy, frequency and the gentle vibration of this love. This energy is available to us at all times. We can access it and switch it on, just like an inverter. I call it the Love Inverter. We can switch it on wherever and whenever love is needed. In fact, it should be always on. We will attract miracles in our life, bringing joy and happiness wherever we go. We are indeed are the very embodiments of love, *'Premasvaruplara'*, as addressed by Sri Sathya Sai Baba, the *Premavatar* (incarnation of love) Himself.

CHAPTER 37: LOVE, THE ESSENCE OF LIFE

The future is an illusion. The reality of the Self, the truth of the Self presents itself, manifests itself and is available to all of us in the present moment only and this presence of the Self can only be experienced. It cannot be known by the mind because the mind does not have the faculty of experiencing. The mind only has the faculty of knowing. It doesn't know things as they are; it knows through its preconceived filter of ideas, opinions, judgements and experiences. We all receive things based on how ready we are. Most of us receive things from our mind and, therefore, without our knowing, we automatically see, hear and experience only the filtered version. We don't even get to know how quickly the mind has tricked us.

There are so many messages that float on social media. We only react to the ones that please our intellect or please our state. That happens when we are still anchored in the mind. However, the heart, which is where the true being lies, sees and experiences everything and everyone as they are. Therefore, the heart is not known to be good with words. It can only emote. It can only express itself through a certain energy which has a vibration and that vibration, which brings such stillness in our body, cannot be put into words. It is a beautiful, lazy, warm feeling where we just want to be. Yet, the energy is so overpowering that it flows through us and, without our knowing, without the mind actually ever getting involved, it reaches out to everybody around us.

That's the beauty of this language of the heart, this expression of love. It has its own way to communicate with all the people around us, with all the beings which we cannot see, with all the residents of the plant world and the animal world. It reaches out to all of them. It travels; it moves and that moves something inside of us as well. We have experienced this in our meditations as well.

By now, we know that there are two worlds, the world of the mind and that of the heart. We have experienced both. With great difficulty, with the grace of the *Guru* and with our yearning, our faith, our determination and our devotion, we have experienced the world of the heart. Till a short while back, we were all residents of the world of the mind. We have seen what it means to be in the world of the mind and in the world of the heart. All agony, all suffering, all pain, all judgements, all expectations and all sorrows exist in the plane of the world of mind. The world of heart does not know any of these, because it operates out of one Consciousness, out of oneness, while the world of the mind operates out of duality, out of separation. Within us, there is no separation, within us there is a whole world and within us lies the whole of existence.

Until some time back, we were part of the world of the mind. We suffered the cross of ignorance, the cross that Jesus Christ had to carry on his shoulders. That cross of ignorance lies like a curse in the world of the mind. It is imperative that we, who have escaped that world and have experienced the world of the heart and the magic and sweetness of love, share this experience for the sake of our brothers and sisters, for the sake of our loved ones.

We are duty bound, because love is compassion, love is selflessness, love goes beyond the boundaries of 'me' and 'mine'. Love shares, love cares, love is the reason for this existence and love is the reason why we were chosen to be given this experience. However, this love is not ours. It's for us to experience, for us to play with and for us to enjoy. Keep in mind that it is a flow. If you try to stop this flow, it will carry you away, because this flow cannot be stopped. Therefore, it has to be shared. It knows no obstructions, it knows no boundaries, it knows no challenges. It has the ability to dissolve and break the toughest of resistance. It has the ability to carry everyone and everything along, just like the river Ganges, just like the mother that carries us in her lap and doesn't mind how heavy we are. She simply carries us along.

That's the power of love. That's the power of the Self. For love, there is no difficult task to accomplish. This path of love is the only path that can join the two worlds. As we share this love with all those who are trapped in the world of the mind, this will come as a breath of fresh air, as a great joy to the ones who are trapped. They are gasping for breath. They are grasping for love. Each one will rise up like a messiah to share this love. This path of love is a pathless path, because it does not leave any footprints behind. It does not create any rigidity or fixation. It works around and it carries everyone along, no matter whether they belong to a particular sect or religion or whether they are atheists. Love is experienced by all. By all I mean human beings, animals and plants. All respond to love.

Love is the natural state of everyone, but all species have been just loving their own. This love that we are now bringing changes the definition of love, because it understands that there is only One, which means we are all tied with this bond of oneness. Therefore, this love is universal. The love that pours out of my heart is not different from the love in your heart and, since this love is common, we are one. It is this oneness which is present in everyone, whether we are inhabitants of the world of heart or the world of the mind. In our oneness, we walk on The Pathless Path - the path of love. From now on, the journey is not outwards but only inwards. From within, everything will happen as it must. Just let go, remain in the flow and let love guide the way forever.

CHAPTER 38: STHITAPRAJNA OR EQUANIMITY

The Bhagavad Gita calls the state of equanimity a state of being balanced and in control within, *Sthitaprajna*. It is a state where we stop reacting to the urges of the mind, to the pinpricks of life and to the people around us, and we start to respond from forgiveness and love, because we are in a state of choiceless awareness and acceptance. We accept that life is as it is. In its imperfection, it is perfect. It was designed to be imperfect so that we could become perfect. It's not that suddenly everything in our life becomes perfect. Perfection of the Self means that we are operating out of our love centre, we experience only love around us, and we are sharing this love with everyone. Once we reach that state, it starts to shift everything. And, as soon as our energy shifts, all the dark energies, the dense people and the heavy things in our life automatically shift. We are no longer given to reactions. We no longer experience extreme anger, jealousy or any kind of strong likings or attachments. We move away from these strong reactions that have been there in our life and we become centred and calm. We experience something that makes us softer within, which is love.

All our reactions were coming from the mind. We did not like anybody to disapprove of us, we always wanted to defend ourselves and prove that we were right. But now, we no longer have a point to prove, because we have got the magic *Mantras* of acceptance, forgiveness and love. We have the awareness of our Truth. We are bringing the cup of happiness into our life; the balance is happening out of gratitude. Since we have shifted, automatically the world around us also has to shift. This is so because the whole world around us is a projection of our mind. Now, we are not operating from our mind but from our heart centre, from the world of love (heart). The old world of the mind holds no meaning anymore, so now our energy becomes so beautiful that all those who have these strong energies will start to either change or become repelled and will move away, when they come into our aura.

The sense of balance, of always being in control of our emotions and our reactions, heightens our sense of awareness. We know that we are operating out of Consciousness when we are fully aware. That awareness is like a powerful searchlight which falls on whatever we are doing. It's as if things start to become amplified in front of us, as if they are put under a microscope and suddenly start to become very big. When we perform our work with that kind of awareness and complete focus, we start to see things which we have not seen before. The little imperfections now start to get highlighted, and a sense of perfection creeps into whatever work we do.

It's really funny how it happens! I'll give you my favourite example. Every day, when I'm cutting vegetables, I have the choice to cut them perfectly or not, especially while chopping onions that make me cry. Still, I want to make sure that the cut is perfect. We begin to see these small little things and they start to become big. When making a cup of tea, that cup of tea has to brew exactly to the right colour and the drops of milk have to be just right. I'm giving small, daily examples. When we are mopping our home, even if there is one small hair, we want to pick it up and put it aside. Things that we didn't notice before suddenly become so visible and obvious to us that we know we have to do something about it. It's as if we were cutting grass with small scissors instead of using a lawn mower. That's how perfect we start becoming.

This happens because our consciousness has shifted and our awareness has expanded. Our awareness is very powerful but, when we are thinking of many things, it loses its power and focus. Therefore, if we are cooking, but thinking of something else, the energy of those thoughts go into our food. If we are driving and our mind is somewhere else, we are not fully conscious. So that is the connection between awareness and perfection.

Perfection is an attitude. No task by itself is perfect or imperfect. Perfection comes when we are in a state of equanimity, when we are absolutely in balance, not troubled by any thought or desire, and we are operating out of stillness and experiencing the sweetness of love inside of us. While writing notes, notice how our handwriting starts to improve when we are balanced, and starts to go bad when we are irritated and agitated. These seem to be little things, but life is only about small little things. It is about what is happening to us right now, at this moment. When we add many small things together, it becomes a big life.

We cannot be perfect if we are not equanimous. We cannot be equanimous if we are not operating out of love. We cannot be in a state of love if we have not experienced stillness in our heart, and we cannot be still unless there is full acceptance in us. We have been picking up every element mentioned and knitting this fabric of life. We have been picking up the threads of life going horizontally and the ones going vertically. When these come together, they make the fabric of life and this is really what Consciousness is about. We should be able to understand Consciousness in our practical day-to-day life.

Till now, we have not touched the concept of God in discussions like 'where He is, where He lies', etcetera'. Instead, we have brought the concept of God to our understanding of what life is. Simply put, God is nothing but Consciousness. We cannot see this Consciousness, but we can feel; we cannot see God, but we can feel Him. If we don't like to use the word God, we can call it Consciousness, *Brahman* or *Atman*. We can also call it love, we can call it miracle, we can call it magic, we can call it synchronicity. We can coin any name, according to what we like. Bhagavad Gita, our holy scripture, also explains everything about this Supreme Consciousness and how to attain it. We too have covered all the concepts in a way that relates to our life and to who we truly are. We now understand all of them, having broached them slowly, methodically and systematically.

Useful Tips

Do not let go of the gift of *Manana* and *Nididhyasana*. Keep marinating yourself in whatever thought you pick up; keep analysing and reflecting upon it. Now that the heart *chakra* is activated and we are operating from there, we will grasp things much better than before. Earlier, the mind was an obstruction, but now it has fallen in sync with the heart. Also, you have all the tools; so, when something happens, you know exactly what to do. Therefore, be stable, be happy, be in a state of equilibrium, and be balanced.

CHAPTER 39: NIRVANA SHATAKAM

Welcome to the penultimate day of the *Atma Chalisa Parayanam*. We have gone through the 'Nine Steps to Divinity' in detail. The ultimate experience of bliss is coming from the sweetness of our love. We feel being in control, equal minded and now look forward to life with enthusiasm, without having any particular choice or will, and ever ready for the Consciousness to guide and show us the way. We are ever prepared, without any expectations or goals, living in the moment and enjoying this inner state of bliss.

When I wrote the book 'Nine Steps to Divinity', I was inspired to include the Nirvana Shatakam at the end, because it is the highest ode to the non-dual Self. It is considered the crest jewel of Advaita Vedanta. At the tender age of eight, Sri Adi Shankaracharya ji went to the mountains in search of his *Guru* or Master and eventually met him. When the Master, Sri Govind Pada, asked him who he was, he answered in six verses (*Shatakam*) to explain the concept of the Self. As it has been the case with a lot of writings in the Vedas, he used the methodology of *Neti Neti* (not this, not this) to describe the state of 'Who am I'. 99.99 percent of the people in this world operate from the mind; so, to be able to express the esoteric concept of consciousness and make it relatable to them, he used the methodology of *Neti Neti*. He looked at every aspect of human existence, negated all that was not the Self and reinforced in the last line of every verse who he really was. After saying what he was not, he tried to always emphasise who he truly was.

So, let's look at what Nirvana Shatakam is expressing, recalling also all that we have discussed during these 38 days.

We will be able to find our checkpoints of the progress we have made in this journey. Since each one of us is on a unique journey, we alone know where we are. Some of us are still on the intellectual side, asking questions which are the basic fundamentals of duality. Some of us are on the intermediate step, some have almost reached the point of experiencing the Self and some are already experiencing it.

Therefore, I would like you to keep mentally doing this self-evaluation as we go into each verse. That's how I understood Nirvana Shatakam before I started to write about it. When Sri Shankaracharya ji speaks about each of the things that he is not, I brought my awareness to those points and I could go deep inside. Actually, there was something in me which was able to take out my blockages and remove the ignorance around it. It just got imprinted in me that 'I am not this'. It really helped me on this path. I know that, as long as this body of mine is here to carry out its *Dharma* (duty), Nirvana Shatakam is going to be a central part of my journey, for the Master had said to me, 'Make sure that everybody knows and understands Nirvana Shatakam'. It is a summary, a conclusion of all that we have been discussing over these past days. To my mind, it is a fitting tribute, not only to the great Master, but to the whole philosophy of Advaita Vedanta and the understanding of the Self.

So, let's start with the first verse,
Mano buddhi ahankara chittani naham
Na cha shrotravjihve na cha ghraana netre
Na cha vyoma bhumir na tejo na vayuhu
Chidananda rupah shivo'ham shivo'ham

In the first verse, Shankaracharya ji picks up the mind aspect and says, 'I am neither the mind (*Manas*) nor the *Buddhi* (intellect), nor the ego (*Ahankara*) nor the *Chitta* which holds the memories in the conscious mind and the subconscious mind.' He says, 'This is not who I am.' I am not going into details but rather giving an overview of the significance of what he is sharing with us. In the second line of the first verse, he says, 'I am neither the five sense organs nor the senses attached to them'. So, just in the first two lines, he has completely detached himself from anything that is happening in the external world, because the external world is a projection of both the mind and the five sense organs. It is clear that he has taken the whole idea of duality out of us.

Then, he says, *Na Cha Vyoma Bhoomir Na Tejo Na Vayu*. He talks about the five elements and says, 'I am neither space, nor earth, nor fire, nor air.' We know this world and the whole universe are made up of five elements. He mentions only four because the poetry has been written to only allow space for four. As when he talked about the sense organs, he actually spoke about four, though he is implying five. Here, he is talking about four elements: space, earth, fire and air, but doesn't talk about water. What he's trying to say is, 'I have nothing to do with this external world as we experience it; I am not any of these elements.' Even our body is made up of these five elements, so that also gets negated. Threrefore, after saying very clearly what he is not, he ends up by saying, '*Chidananda Rupa Shivoham Shivoham* - I am *Chid Ananda*'. *Chid* is the awareness of Consciousness, which is bestowing bliss on us. Therefore, he is saying, 'I am that Existence, Consciousness and Bliss. I am Shiva, I am Shiva. I am love, light and Consciousness.' Shiva is also called *Bhole Baba* (Innocent). He is very innocent, he is full of love, he has no interest in interfering with what's happening in the world. He sits in Kailasa, in a beautiful meditative pose, and is in love with the whole of Creation. He himself is Consciousness. He wears ash on his head because he is completely detached and is always in this state of bliss. So, that's how Shiva is introduced and that's who we all are- Existence, Consciousness and Bliss. All of us are Shiva. He is neither masculine nor feminine. Shiva is a state of consciousness, a state of being.

The second verse says,
Na Cha Prana Sangyo Na Vai Pancha Vayu
Na Va Saptadhatur Na Va Pancha Koshah
Na Vak Pani Padau Na Chopastha Payu
Chidananda Rupa Shivoham Shivoham

Again, he goes into each element and says, 'I am neither the vital breath that I take nor the *Pancha Pranas* (five airs of *Prana, Apana, Udana, Vyana* and *Samana* in our body); I am none of these, because they are all in the body and I am not the body.' Then, he says, 'I am not the *Saptadhatu* (the seven body tissues of plasma, blood, muscles, adipose tissue, bones, bone marrow and reproductive tissues) nor the *Pancha Koshas* (five sheaths).' The first sheath is our gross body, which is made out of food, *Annamaya Kosha*. He goes into all that the body is made up of and says, I am not this. He also says, 'I am not the *Manomaya kosha* or mind, nor the *Vijnanamaya Kosha* or higher intellect, nor the *Anandmaya Kosha* or bliss sheath'. In a minute, Sri Shankaracharya ji says, 'I am neither the five *Koshas,* nor the seven tissues of the body nor the seven elements of the body.' Then, he says, '*Na Vak Pani Padau Na Chopastha Payu*, I am not the five instruments of speaking, grasping, motion, elimination and procreation.' He dissociates himself from all the organs of action and from all the actions performed by these organs. At the end, he again says, 'I am Existence, Consciousness and Bliss. I am Shiva, I am Shiva. I am pure love and Consciousness.'

The third verse says,
Na Me Dvesha Ragau Na Me Lobha Mohau
Mado Naiva Me Naiva Matsarya Bhavah
Na Dharmo Na Chartho Na Kamo Na Mokshah
Chidananda Rupa Shivoham Shivoham

He has realised, 'I am neither *Dvesha* (dislike or revulsion), nor the sense of liking, meaning neither do I hate anyone nor I am particularly fond or attached to anything or anyone.' When we get close to somebody, in the beginning, we like them a lot and start getting attached. As we come closer, we begin to see their weaknesses and start to experience dislike, which can turn into revulsion and even into hatred. These are the feelings that we move between in life, the likes and dislikes. Then he says, '*Na Me Lobha Mohau*, I am not the feeling of greed or attachment.' We know that all these four feelings come from the mind. We like, we dislike, we get greedy about some things or we get attached to people. So, the feeling part is now also beginning to be negated. '*Mado Naiva Me Naiva Matsarya Bhavah*, I am not the feeling of jealousy nor of pride, nor do I suffer from these because I do not compete with anybody, as there is only one Consciousness.' Since he doesn't see any separation, he says he is not suffering from any of these maladies.

Our Vedas talk about the four goals of life, *Dharma, Artha, Kama* and *Moksha. Dharma* is what we do in life. We spend our time earning money and wealth to use it for righteousness or for supporting the goodness principle. *Kama* (desire) is to run after the attractions of life, which have to do with the five senses and the five organs of action. Shankaracharya ji says, *Na Dharmo Na Chartho Na Kamo Na Mokshah*. After running after all this, we come to the last state which is *Moksha* (liberation). '*Moha*' is attachment or desire, and '*Ksha*' is to give up all attachment to worldly desires. So, first we run after desires and wealth and then, in the last part of our life, we try to get rid of them. Shankaracharya ji says, 'I am neither seeking *Moksha* nor I am running after *Kama*, nor do I have any *Dharma* to perform. I am way beyond all this and, therefore, these four goals of life are no longer relevant to me. They are relevant to a human body but I am not this body. I am *Chidananda Rupa Shivoham Shivoham*.' Systematically, each idea about life that we took from our scriptures or from our concepts of religion is negated in the first three verses.

Then, he moves to the 4th verse that says,

Na Punyam Na Papam Na Saukhyam Na Dukham
Na Mantro Na Teertham Na Vedo Na Yajnaha
Aham Bhojanam Naiva Bhojyam Na Bhokta
Chidananda Rupa Shivoham Shivoham

'I am not caught up in the idea of *Punyam* and *Papam*, of doing meritorious or good deeds, neither am I affected by the idea of sin or guilt.' *Na Saukhyam Na Dukham*, means, 'I am neither enjoying any comforts because of my past good *Karmas*, nor I am suffering from any *Dukham*, pain, suffering or sorrow, because I am not part of these cycles that only affect the human body; I am not the human body'. Then, he says *Na Mantro Na Teertham Na Vedo Na Yajnaha*. He is declaring, 'I have no sacred hymn to chant, neither I am impacted by the benefits of any *Mantra*, nor do I go to any pilgrimages or perform any rituals. For me, there are no holy places, since everything is auspicious and divine. So, how can there be a bad place and a good place? Also, there is no concept of Vedas for me. Vedas have all the knowledge that has first to be consumed by the mind, and I am not impacted by any of that. All the knowledge of the Vedas is useless for me because it is for a person who is bound and wants to get free; and I am already a free spirit. I do not have to perform any *Yajna* (sacrificial rite) because that is based on the concept of duality that there are some gods to propitiate and please. Since I am one Consciousness, I have no need of performing any of these sacrifices.'

Then he says, '*Aham Bhojanam Naiva Bhojyam Na Bhokta*, I am neither the experience nor the experienced nor the experiencer. I am not the subject of that which needs to be enjoyed, nor I am the enjoyed nor I am the enjoyer'. He's saying that, if we were to eat some food, we are neither the person who eats the food, nor the food, nor the enjoyer of the food. We are not associated with any consumption whatsoever, either through the five senses or the five organs of action. 'I am *Chidananda Rupam Shivoham Shivoham.*'

Then he comes to the fifth verse that says,
Na Me Mrityu Shanka Na Me Jati Bhedah
Pita Naiva Me Naiva Mata Na Janma
Na Bandhur Na Mitram Gurur Naiva Shishyah
Chidananda Rupa Shivoham Shivoham

'*Na Me Mrityu Shanka*- I have no fear of death nor do I have death, because death only comes to the body. Where is the question of the fear of death when I was never born nor will I ever die?' As we have discussed in the past, death is the mother of all fears. Whatever fears and insecurities we have inside of us, the root cause of all of them is death. So, he says there is no question of death or of having any fear of death because I am not the body. '*Na Me Jati Bhedah*. I do not have any caste or creed because there is no separation.' Whether you are born in a higher caste or a lower caste, either by birth or by your actions, there is no difference whatsoever.

Then he says, '*Pita Naiva Me Naiva Mata Na Janma*, I do not have any father nor any mother, nor did I ever take birth, since birth and all these relationships are of the body.' How many mothers and fathers have we had in countless lifetimes? Since we don't remember any of those, even those who we have right now are also not part of who we are because we've never belonged to them. In the next line, he talks about other relationships. '*Na Bandhur Na Mitram Gurur Naiva Shishyah*, I do not have brothers or friends, neither do I have a *Guru* nor any disciple.' He is simply taking away all the relationships that exist. All relationships are connected to the body. They come about by birth, by what we do and by our connections with people around us. So, he says that all those are not who he is. Remember, he's telling his *Guru* who he is and, in defining that, he is destroying the entire edifice of duality based on the body and the mind, the senses and the organs of action. He has completely decimated the whole idea of being a name and a body, *Nama-Rupa* (name and form).

After saying *Neti Neti,* he comes to what he really wants to say. In the sixth verse, he very simply describes who he is,

Aham Nirvikalpo Nirakara Roopaha
Vibhur Vyapya Sarvatra Sarvendriyanam
Sada Me Samatvam Na Muktir Na Bandhah
Chidananda Rupa Shivoham Shivoham

'*Aham* (I am) *Nirvikalpo* (choiceless). I have no choice of my own, I have no *Vikalp* (volition), no particular mindset whatsoever, so I am choiceless. *Nirakara Roopaha* (I have no form) because I am pure Consciousness. I have no form, no body, so I have no attributes. I have no qualities because I am that pure energetic Principle. *Vibhur Vyapya Sarvatra Sarvendriyanam,* I am present everywhere, I am pervading everything, I am ever present as the conscious energetic principle. *Na Muktir Na Bandhah,* since I am present everywhere, since I am in everything and since I am this pure Consciousness which is ever present, free flowing as the love consciousness principle, I am neither bound nor I am liberated. Where is the question of looking for liberation, when I was never bound? My binding was all coming from the mind, from my wrong understanding that I am this name and this body. Therefore, this name and this body created the entire projection of *Jagat* (world).'

We started off by saying *Brahma Sathya Jagat Mithya,* this world is just a projection, an illusion. It is not real. What is real is Brahman, the energetic principle, the love Consciousness principle, the Shiva principle, Consciousness. When we experience that, it gives us the feeling of bliss, which is uninterrupted and permanent joy, which is not subject to death, destruction or decay, which never dies, which was never born, which was never bound and, therefore, there is no question of liberation or of freedom. I am *Chidananda Rupa Shivoham Shivoham.*

That is the journey we have had over these 39 days of

Parayanam. As we come to the end of this journey, we pay our tribute to Lord Shiva.

CHAPTER 40: AHAM BRAHMASMI

Welcome to the day of celebration, the final day of our *Parayanam*. I want to thank Sri Sathya Sai Baba for this inspiration and all the Masters, who are the embodiments of Consciousness, for guiding us throughout to make it an experiential journey. And I want to thank all of you who have participated and energetically co-created this holy *Parayanam*.

All is perfect; all is absolutely as it must be. On this journey, we have experienced that everything is as it is meant to be, in whatever state it is. You can call it imperfection, madness, or chaos. It is how the world is at this point in time because that is how it is meant to be at this time. In these forty days, we have also experienced that the outer world is a mere projection, a mere play of all the past *Karmas*. Somewhere throughout, there is the dance of Consciousness going on.

We keep enjoying and suffering the world based on our own perceptions and how we see things through our mind. We have our eyes, but they see objects only physically. It is actually the mind that controls what we see, how we see, how we perceive and what we make of it. Therefore, this is a make-believe world wherein all of us participate, yet our worldviews are very different. This happens because we've been looking at the world through our own filters, based on our experiences, our *Vasanas* (past impressions), our *Prarabhda Karmas* (accumulated *Karmas* of past lives), and our *Gunas* (qualities). In this journey, we have realised that we are not the mind and the body, but the Consciousness that is within us, which is present everywhere and is known by many names: God, Brahman, *Atman*, Self, Consciousness and many more. We have the freedom to call it whatever we want; the idea is to experience it. Names and appearances can be misleading, but the experience is our very own. Our ability to see the difference between the experiences of the mind and the experiences of Consciousness or the heart clearly gives us the discrimination that enables us to remain in the awareness of that Consciousness.

In the Vedas and the Upanishads, there are four *Mahavakyas* (exhortations) that describe the Self. The first one is *Prajnanam Brahma* (Consciousness is Brahman). *Prajnanam Brahma* is the Consciousness that we have been talking about over this entire journey. The second *Mahavakya* says *Ayam Atma Brahma*, meaning that this *Atma*, which is inside of me as the individual entity, is also Brahman. So, consciousness is Brahman, which is all-pervading and the *Atman*, which resides in the individual, is also Brahman. This leads to the third *Mahavakya- Tat Tvam Asi* (Thou art That) which is the Oneness principle, which means, 'You and I are one'. This means that the same Consciousness that is inside of me is also inside of you, and therefore we are one; there is the same Consciousness inside each of us. These are the three instructive statements which clarify that what we call God, Consciousness, Brahman, or *Atman* are one and the same; the same consciousness is inside all of us, so we are one. Knowing that we undertake our journey in life so that we can discover it for ourselves and experience it firsthand, to gain the direct experience or *Pratyaksha Pramana*. When we get this direct experience of Consciousness within, which is the goal of the *Parayanam,* it is called *Aham Brahmasmi*, the fourth *Mahavakya*.

In this *Parayanam,* when we came to the state of beingness, we suddenly started to experience its symptoms and signs. Each one of us started to have experiences, and we realised how sweet the experience of Consciousness is and what stillness we go into when we experience it. Our life becomes a song of love that flows from us and is received by everyone around us, not just by human beings but by all beings, including animals and plants. Since all living beings also operate out of the

Consciousness of love, they all have the ability to receive and to give love, because that is the basic energy.

This Brahman, this God, this *Guru*, this inner *Guru*, relates to us and interacts with each one of us as love. We experience that presence as love which is selfless, which flows, which makes us do things because we know we must do them, and which transcends all the notions and the boundaries set up by the mind. It breaks all the matrices that we were stuck with in our life, either by compulsion, circumstances or choice. We realise that everything in our life has been created by our mind, and we have always been its prisoners. However, when this love starts to flow and prompts us to do things, and we do them, then we instantly know that we have moved beyond and left that world of the mind behind. The mind will continue to do its work. Without mind, we cannot exist; but the steering wheel of our life moves from the mind to the Consciousness and an inner language, an inner dialogue starts for all of us.

This inner dialogue comes to us in the form of intuition. We get an intuitive ability that prompts us to do certain things, and we wonder at the synchronicity that starts happening. Synchronicity is the way Consciousness validates that something is not a coincidence, that everything is happening as per a higher plan (the plan of Consciousness), and therefore things start to flow. When the flow is not there, we know that Consciousness is trying to tell us that we are operating out of the mind. Another way Consciousness communicates to us what we need to do or take note of, is through dreams. We know when dreams are messages of Consciousness and when they are just the clearing out of the subconscious. We are able to differentiate because Consciousness, the observer of these dreams, instantly knows what the dream is about. As this Consciousness is not attached to the world in the waking state, it is also not attached to the observations of the dreams. It sees them as communication, receives the communication, does what it needs to do, but does not build any attachment because both the waking state and the dream state are an illusion, a part of the grand *Maya*.

Another way we have been experiencing how Consciousness shows its presence is through energetic experiences, because ultimately Consciousness is an energy. We are now able to identify how it feels and what it is like. We cannot see electricity, but we can perceive it through the bulb, the tube, and the fan that works. So, we can feel that electricity is there through all these various appliances. Likewise, we cannot see God but are able to experience the presence of this Consciousness through multiple ways. The experience of stillness makes us feel connected to it at all times and we are aware of it at all times. So, Consciousness is also a constant integrated awareness. And, in this awareness lies all the qualities of creation and its creator.

This awareness makes us flow through life. We experience love as a gentle sweetness in our heart, and that gives us a feeling of being enthusiastic towards life because we start separating ourselves from the mind and the body. The joy in our hearts does not diminish, even if there are challenges happening to the body or if the mind is trying to distract us. As an example, during this 40-day period, many experienced a lot of clearing. Some experienced fever, some experienced back problems, and some went through a particularly rough patch at home or at work. Yet, whatever happened to the body, whatever experiences one had, the awareness of that presence or the joy in their heart never diminished. They held on, and they knew how to see the body and the mind for what it really is.

In the end, how do we know that we are operating from Consciousness? It is when we start to experience the flow of love from us, when we start interacting with people out of love, when our strong reactions melt away and equanimity becomes our hallmark while we deal with situations and people in life. Our awareness expands so much that we are able to do even the smallest jobs perfectly, and life becomes a flow of *Saral* (simple) and *Sahaja* (natural). Everything becomes very simple, uncomplicated, natural, and spontaneous. The resultant experiences are of deep peace or *Shanti,* and we feel content or *Santosh.* Remember, the wise words of Sage Vashishta regarding the four sentinels guarding the world of Self-realisation. They are *Satsanga* (company of seekers of truth), *Vichara* (contemplation / *Manana*), *Santosh* (contentment) and *Shanti* (peace). We've spoken about all of them, and we've been practising *Manana* over the last 40 days. Now, what we experience in this *Satsanga* is contentment and peace.

So, this experience, this feeling, is of *Aham Brahmasmi,* that I am that Brahman. This is the fourth *Mahavakya.* These *Mahavakyas* are very difficult to understand, but we have put them down into very clear simple indicators to which we can now relate. When we are not experiencing it, we instantly know that our mind is hijacking us or diverting us somewhere else. Like a torch, awareness will no longer let us forget it. It will certainly and instantly get switched on whenever there is darkness. This darkness is the darkness of thoughts and desires that the mind pulls us into. As we start to fall for it, the awareness comes; when anger or jealousy starts to come, we suddenly realise that something is brewing up; when we're getting attached to someone or something, suddenly the awareness will come and tell us that we are getting attached to this. It is with constant *Abhyasa* (practice of remaining in this awareness) that a day comes when we are always in this state and, no matter what happens, this state does not get perturbed. We do not feel upset; we do not lose it, and that is when we truly become *Jivanmuktas* -liberated beings or *yogis*- who have mastered the art of being equanimous in the chaotic world that surrounds us.

It is here where our work really starts. While we say that

Self-realisation or experiencing Brahman is the goal of our life, I would like to tell you that it's another illusion because that is when our work really starts. That is when we finally start living who we truly are. Finally, when we experience it and come into that state of joy, that is when the real fun of life starts. Why would we want to let it go, why would we want to rest? The joy is so beautiful that we must share it with others. What we experience (this joy), we cannot keep it to ourselves. It becomes our bounden duty to share this joy with others. This is the nature of joy, this is what *Ananda* is; and it comes only once we constantly remain in the presence of our Truth.

So, that's the conclusion of this *Parayanam*. I wanted to make sure that we completely understand the journey that we have made. We started off talking about the nine steps to Divinity and we said our aim was to experience the flow of love which would give us the experience of Bliss. That we have done. Today we have summarised and recapped everything once again, so that it is not left to our imagination what this experience is. We know all the indicators now, we know how it feels having experienced it ourselves.

Useful Tips

I hope everybody has maintained a journal, as it is going to be your most invaluable asset and companion for the rest of your life, since you have noted down your experiences and your progress over these 40 days. From time to time, you should look at it to realise how you have shifted, how things moved, when did the penny drop, when did that joy start to come and what were your key learnings. You must practise all your learnings, else later you might not be able to relate to them and also lose the state of awareness. In such a case, the journal will always help you to come back into your true state of being.

APPENDIX

THE CUP OF HAPPINESS

In Chapter 31, we covered the Cup Of Happiness. Below is a chart that goes along with that chapter which gives you the Recipe for Perfect Happiness.

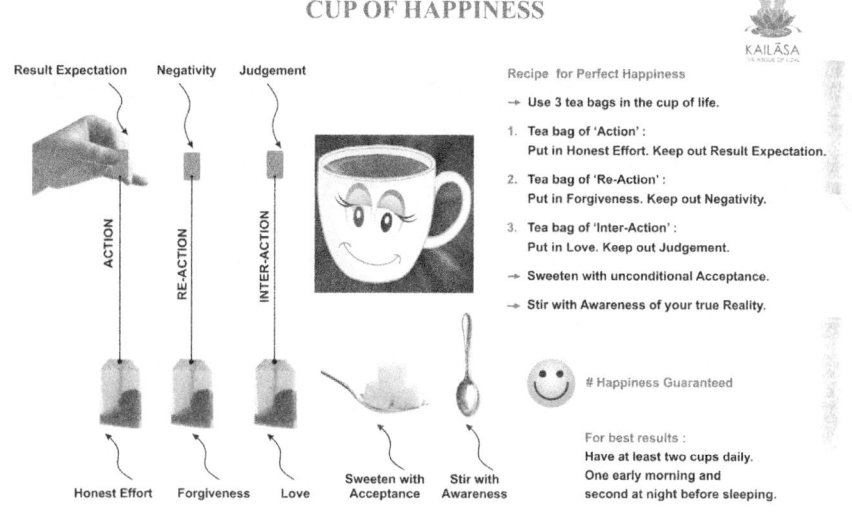

CUP OF HAPPINESS

Result Expectation　Negativity　Judgement

ACTION　RE-ACTION　INTER-ACTION

Honest Effort　Forgiveness　Love　Sweeten with Acceptance　Stir with Awareness

KAILĀSA

Recipe for Perfect Happiness

→ Use 3 tea bags in the cup of life.

1. Tea bag of 'Action' :
   Put in Honest Effort. Keep out Result Expectation.

2. Tea bag of 'Re-Action' :
   Put in Forgiveness. Keep out Negativity.

3. Tea bag of 'Inter-Action' :
   Put in Love. Keep out Judgement.

→ Sweeten with unconditional Acceptance.

→ Stir with Awareness of your true Reality.

Happiness Guaranteed

For best results :
Have at least two cups daily.
One early morning and
second at night before sleeping.

TRIKUTI

In this book we have also referred to the *Trikuti*. This technique has been taught by Swami Rama of the Himalayan Tradition. The *Guru Chakra* or *Jnana Chakra* dispels the darkness of ignorance by bringing in light of knowledge. The Fire of Knowledge is the Highest Fire that purifies all negativity. The Fire of Knowledge is located at the *TRIKUTI*. *Trikuti* means a triangle that has 3 equal sides. Using the *Trikuti* we can remove all negative thoughts and emotions and cleanse our subconscious.

You can find a video on our Tube Channel which explains how to practise this technique. You will find this video at:

https://www.youtube.com/watch?v=xbBiUBJEsfQ&t=2s

WEESITE:
KAILASALOVE.COM

YOU TUBE:
KAILASA THE ABODE OF LOVE
FACEBOOK:
KAILASA THE ABODE OF LOVE
INSTAGRAM:
KAILASA_THE_ABODE_OF_LOVE
BLOG:
VIKASNIRVANA.WORDPRESS.COM

Printed in Great Britain
by Amazon